A CHIP OFF THE OLD BLACK

A CHIP
OFF THE
OLD BLACK

Arthur Black

HARBOUR PUBLISHING

1 2 3 4 5 — 14 13 12 11 10

Harbour Publishing Co. Ltd.
P.O. Box 219, Madeira Park, BC, V0N 2H0
www.harbourpublishing.com

Edited by Margaret Tessman.
Cover photograph by Howard Fry.
Printed and bound in Canada.

Harbour Publishing acknowledges financial support from the Government
of Canada through the Canada Book Fund and the Canada Council for
the Arts, and from the Province of British Columbia through the BC Arts
Council and the Book Publishing Tax Credit.

Library and Archives Canada Cataloguing in Publication

Black, Arthur
        A chip off the old Black / Arthur Black.

ISBN 978-1-55017-510-3

        1. Canadian wit and humor (English). I. Title.

PS8553.L318C55 2010   C818'.5402   C2010-904113-5

To Jimbo
(he ain't heavy, he's my brother)

CONTENTS

PART ONE

UP, UP AND AWAY!

HE'S ALIVE!
ISN'T THAT AMAZING?

So you look at your mug grinning back at you from the bathroom mirror and you think you're Pretty Hot Stuff.

You wound up with the spouse of your dreams, a home your enemies would grow envy ulcers to see, three picture-perfect kids, a hybrid in the garage and a sizeable wad in the bank. Your health is good, nobody wants to outright kill you and your biggest addiction is the Sudoku puzzle in the newspaper.

Yup, you tell your mirror image, I'm leading a pretty full life.

Think so? Meet Brian Keating.

He's a mid-life guy. And noticeably bright-eyed, dark-haired and slim. We'd be slim too, if we burned calories like he does. His business card reads "Head of Conservation Outreach, Calgary Zoo." It would be simpler and more accurate if it just carried the lyrics of the old Hank Snow song: "I've been everywhere."

Haida Gwaii? Of course. Ellesmere Island? Walked across it. High Arctic? Lived there. Antarctic? Too many times to count. Africa? More than forty visits.

This is a guy who felt vexed hiking the Rockies because high above he could see inaccessible valleys and meadows only mountain goats could reach. So he got a pilot's licence in order to fly to them. He's climbed Kilimanjaro and scuba dived in the Sargasso Sea. He's played patty cakes with penguins and paddled with narwhals. Once, his kayak was T-boned and cut in two—by a grumpy hippo.

And he's been unarmed and face-to-fangs with a very large and very hostile African male lion. "Didn't know I could run backward that fast," he says. "Didn't know anyone could."

So who is this guy—Steve Irwin North? Tarzan of the Tundra? A Stampede version of Crocodile Dundee?

Nope. He started out as curator of the Calgary Zoo in 1981, but it wasn't long before he was packing his rucksack. Backroom cataloguing and dusty dioramas held no magic for Keating. Nowadays, when he's not in the jungle or up a mountain or out on an ice floe, chances are you'll find him showing slides of his adventures on some stage to hundreds—sometimes thousands—of armchair adventurer wannabes. He's an international speaker and he's hot—addressing audiences more than sixty times a year. Why? Because Brian Keating is also a salesman—and so positive he makes Don Cherry look like a funeral director. Keating is flogging the natural wonders of the world—not as a tour guide, more as a canary in the mine. He wants everybody to know about what's still left of our wonderful unspoiled earth.

He's no Pollyanna—Keating knows better than most the depredation man's rapaciousness for raw material and bigger backyards has caused (and cost). That's what keeps him on the circuit. To paraphrase the old hymn, his eyes have seen the glory and he wants us to see it too. See it, in order to save it. The signature mantra that he repeats as he shows yet another audience close-ups of lowland gorillas, basking walruses, trumpeting elephants or curious wolves: "Isn't that *amazing?*"

Yes. Yes, it is. And so is Brian Keating. Especially since he really ought to be dead.

Almost was, too—not from the swipe of a lion's paw or a tumble into an alpine crevasse but from the bumper of a car in downtown Calgary. Keating was standing with his bicycle at a stoplight on his way to the CBC TV studio when a car came out of nowhere and creamed him. The collision left him lying in the middle of the road with smashed ribs, a broken arm and some pretty ugly facial injuries. Keating (of course) insists that he was lucky.

"The only thing that saved my life was my bicycle helmet," says

Keating. "It was smashed into about fifty pieces, all the little bits dangling, held together by the chin strap." The hospital staff was so impressed they asked if they could keep the helmet and show it to kids who thought they were too cool to wear bike helmets. Keating said sure—as long as they didn't wash the bloodstains off. "Tell them that's what my skull would have looked like without the helmet," he said.

Classic Keating. And if one day some kid goes over the handlebars, lands on his head and happens, thanks to Keating's example, to be wearing a helmet that saves him from a brain omelette, I know exactly how Keating will respond when he hears about it.

He'll say, "Isn't that *amazing?*"

DUBAI: LOOKING DUBIOUS

So your investments have cratered. Your love life is a sick joke. The car engine makes a funny tickety-ping sound every time you accelerate, there's a brassy taste in the back of your throat when you climb the stairs, your pants don't fit, your Visa's maxed out and there's a note in your inbox saying the boss would like to "have a word" with you after work.

Look on the bright side—at least you're not stuck in Dubai.

Dubai is, not to put too fine a point on it, a mushrooming hell-hole. The bottom of the empty oil barrel. The end of the world. A snake pit, except it's too inhospitable for snakes.

Mind you, that might not be your first impression of the place. Dubai perches on the edge of the Persian Gulf, shimmering out of the Arabian Desert like a shiny, impossible mirage of steel and glass. It has the world's tallest building, a seven-star hotel, a huge seaport, a brand new airport—even its own stock exchange. It has Palm Jumierah Island, a man-made archipelago of sand that added four thousand residences and seventy-eight kilometres to the Dubai coastline—in the form of a colossal palm tree fanning out into the Persian Gulf.

One building, the wretchedly excessive 23 Marina (which may or may not be completed this year), is eighty-nine storeys high. It contains 288 apartments, 57 of which have private swimming pools.

On their balconies.

Not surprisingly for a country where the temperature routinely tops out over 40 degrees Celsius, Dubai has a thing for swimming pools. The Atlantis Hotel, which opened with a launch party costing $20 million (you read right), boasts a whale shark in its swimming pool.

Not so long ago, it was reported that 25 percent of all construction cranes *in the world* were chugging and hoisting away around the clock in Dubai. Workers, from navvies to engineers, streamed in from all over the world—so much so that they outnumbered native Arabs eight to one. The streets were chrome and steel rivers of Hummers and Mercedes. The malls were full of jet-setters and celebrities. And why not? All that oil money, right?

Wrong. Number one: oil prices went south along with the rest of the world economy; and number two: Dubai doesn't have any oil anyway. It relies on real estate and well-heeled tourists—and those are very soft commodities these days. All Dubai's got—when you remove the glitz and gloss—is sand.

The bad economic news is better known outside the city limits than within, because for most of the past two centuries Dubai has been ruled by the iron-fisted and pathologically conservative Al Maktoum family. It is forbidden to bad mouth Dubai in Dubai. You can spend an unspecified length of time in a very nasty jail if you indulge.

But it's not difficult to find yourself on the wrong side of a Dubai jail wall. All you have to do is lose your job. It is illegal—and punishable by imprisonment—to be unemployed in Dubai.

That explains a phenomenon seen more and more in the parking complex of Al Maktoum International Airport. What you find are cars—almost new and obviously abandoned—by workers who've lost their jobs and had no prospects of getting another. Some of the cars have notes of apology taped to their windshields. Their ex-pat owners have fled back from whence they came with whatever they could pack in a suitcase. At last count airport parking stalls held more than three thousand unclaimed vehicles.

Not surprising. Jobs in Dubai that have not outright disappeared have been downsized pay-wise. Just a short while ago a civil engineer with four years' experience could expect to earn 15,000 dirhams a month. Now, the maximum is 8,000 dirhams—about $2,000 US.

Not enough in a town where the rent for even a cheesy apartment can set you back $5,000 a month.

Two hundred years ago the poet Shelley wrote about a vanished desert kingdom once ruled by a "king of kings" named Ozymandias. All that remained of it were "two vast and trunkless legs of stone" and some rubble.

Round the decay of that colossal wreck, boundless and bare
The lone and level sands stretch far away.

Sounds like a pretty fair description of the view from downtown Dubai in the not so distant future.

CANDY OFFENSIVE?
BAH, HUMBUG!

On behalf of all Canadians I would like to extend an apology to New Zealanders, all 4.3 million of them, and that's not counting sheep and kiwis. It concerns an international incident initiated by a Canadian—one Seeka Parsons, of Nunavut. Ms. Parsons, on a visit to New Zealand, chanced to visit a corner store where she beheld, horror of horrors, a candy confection being sold to the public under the name of—be brave, oh typing finger . . .

Eskimos.

That's right—a candy called "Eskimo." It is even in the shape of a person wearing a fur-lined parka. Ms Parsons was appalled to learn that not only was the sale of "Eskimo" candies legal, but New Zealanders had been enthusiastically chowing down on them for the past half century.

Ms. Parsons knew what had to be done. She called a TV station, which led to a press conference at which she denounced the product as an insult to her people. She vowed that she would send packages of the candies back to Prime Minister Stephen Harper as well as to tribal elders in Nunavut. "I just think that we deserve to have respect and by having a lolly or a candy that's made of a whole entire race of people, my people, I right away knew that I had to make a change," she said into the camera of New Zealand's national TV news program.

Actually, they are not made of an entire race of people; they are made of chocolate-covered marshmallow. And they are not genetic beacons, racial signifiers or tundral Arks of the Covenant. These Eskimos are merely candies.

Lots of nationality-branded goodies end up going down the cake hole—Dutch cobbler, Irish coffee, English muffins, German bratwurst, Belgian waffles and French pastries, to name a handful. The peoples so "disrespected" seem to be thriving nicely.

Ms. Parsons claims that even the name is an insult to her people—the Inuit. She says that "Eskimo" was a derogative term appropriated by early white men and that it means "eaters of raw meat"—but the jury's out on that. According to a Smithsonian expert, "Eskimo" means "snowshoe netters"; according to Quebec linguist Jose Mailhot, it means "people who speak a different language." None of it (Nunavut?)—including "eaters of raw meat"—sounds terribly offensive to my ears.

You want offensive, Ms. Parsons? Consider my people—the Scots. We have been reviled down through the ages as kilted crazies, bagpipe buffoons and dour, unsmiling skinflints who could squeeze a Canadian nickel until the beaver wiggled its tail for mercy. Have we ever given the world anything so gastronomically tantalizing as a chocolate-covered marshmallow candy? Och, I wish. We have given the world porridge, Scottish oatcakes and haggis.

Luckily for the PM, we Scots are far too, ah, thrifty, to send him any samples in the mail.

If I could offer two words of advice to Ms. Parsons of Nunavut they would be: "Lighten Up." Food can be fun, you know. Ask Ben and Jerry. That would be Ben Cohen and Jerry Greenfield, two sixties hippies who started an ice cream business with just two rules: it had to taste good and it had to be fun.

And they made it fun. They came up with flavours like Jamaican Me Crazy, Vermonty Python, Mission to Marzipan and, in honour of their favourite band, the Grateful Dead, Cherry Garcia.

Ben and Jerry even managed to have fun with the last hapless occupant of the Oval Office, for whom they felt minimal affection. Still, in honour of George W., they created flavours like: Grape Depression, Chock and Awe, Iraqi Road and imPeachMint.

Not to mention Nougalar Proliferation, Wire Tapioca and Fudgin' da Books.

And here's a gesture that, as a northerner, Ms. Parsons could get behind. On Earth Day in 2005, as a protest against the Bush administration proposal to open the Arctic National Wildlife Refuge to oil drilling, Ben and Jerry's created a humungous dessert and deposited it—all 1,140 pounds worth—in front of the US Capitol Building in Washington.

A baked Alaska, of course.

The last I heard, Cadbury New Zealand, the company that makes the Eskimo candy, had dismissed Ms. Parsons' complaint out of hand. A spokesperson said that they sold nineteen million Eskimos last year and that the candy is "one of our most sought after."

I say, good for Cadbury New Zealand. They recognized the controversy as a mere humbug and wisely decided not to get inuit.

WHOSE BRIGHT IDEA WAS THAT?

An invasion of armies can be resisted, but not an idea whose time has come.

—Victor Hugo

Bang on, Victor. And it's not always new ideas we need. Sometimes we need to take an old idea down to the riverbank and hold it under the water until it stops moving.

Airline tickets for instance. I don't know whose bright idea it was to foist airline tickets on an unsuspecting world, but somewhere between the Wright boys mucking about at Kitty Hawk and the Concorde swooshing across the Atlantic, some airline nimrod decided that no one should be allowed aloft without a sheaf of paper composed of incomprehensible gibberish reproduced in quintuplicate clutched in his fist.

Airline tickets—not a great idea. Too bulky to fit in your pocket and too flimsy to survive rough handling, airline tickets were the last word in pointless paperwork—unless you happened to lose yours.

I did, once. I got to the Air Canada ticket gate in Vancouver for a flight to Kelowna, fanned through my pockets for my ticket—gone, lost, *disparu*. I shrugged apologetically to the ticket agent and prepared to show my ID.

"That'll be ninety dollars," the ticket agent said.

For what? To reprint a piece of paper? Check your computer,

I told the agent. You'll find my name on there. How many Arthur Blacks you figure there are on flight AC 56 to Kelowna?

"Ninety dollars," he said. "Cash or credit card. We don't take cheques."

This ugly scene played out perhaps ten years ago in Vancouver airport. It would never happen today because, at some point in the last decade, someone had the bright idea to replace those dopey wads of paper with e-tickets. It not only removed a source of migraines for travellers, it saved the airlines a bundle of dough. The IATA (International Air Transport Association) estimates it took about ten dollars to process an old-fashioned paper airline ticket. Cost of processing an e-ticket: about a buck. Savings to the industry: $3 billion US a year.

No-brainer.

Here's another no-brainer: hospital gowns.

Of all the humiliations you will endure during your next hospital visit for a checkup—the jabbings, the pokings, the proddings and probings—none will resonate quite as terrifyingly as the dumb-ass gown they will hand you to put on. The adjective is apt. You know the gown I mean. "Take off all your clothes and slip into this," the nurse will smirk. It goes on like an apron, with ties at the neck and the waist. Here's a news flash for the gown designers: All guys—in fact, most people this side of Martha Stewart—are extremely ham-handed when it comes to blindly tying reef knots behind their backs.

And besides, no matter how deftly you tie the knot of a hospital gown, it still leaves most of your caboose hanging out in the breeze.

Whose bright idea was that?

No doctor I have ever questioned could satisfactorily explain the bizarre and composure-rattling construction of this garment. "They've always been like that," is the usual rationalization.

Yeah, well they're not anymore. Some genius, working for the firm MIP Inc. in Montreal, has come up with a replacement they call the "respectful" gown. It's opaque and wraps around the body to cover the backside and tie at the (well, duh!) *front* of the body, rather than at the back.

Which means the patient is not involuntarily mooning everybody standing astern.

The rejigged hospital gown isn't just patient-friendly, it's a boon to hospital budgets as well. Because they're made of microfibre, the new gowns wash easier, dry quicker, last longer and look better. A study conducted at five Quebec hospitals that use the new gowns shows an annual saving of $118,000 just from not having to fold the nine thousand new gowns each time they're washed.

Are the new gowns at your hospital yet? Probably not, but they're on the way. It's just as Victor Hugo said—you can't stop an idea whose time has come.

If Fate should take you to the hospital for a checkup before the new gowns arrive, try to keep your back to the wall. And for God's sake don't bend over to adjust your paper slippers.

OF HAWAII AND HUMPBACKS

A m I the last Canuck to discover the joys of Hawaii? Sure seemed like it after I announced plans to spend a couple of weeks in Maui. Hardly had the H-word crossed my lips when I was inundated with tips from fellow citizens who, as far as I knew, had never ventured beyond the bright lights of Brampton.

"Oh yeah—Maui. Make sure you spend a day on the beach at Ka'anapali. Don't miss 'Ulupalakua or Ke'anae and Wailua. And remember to drive up Haleakala to check out a sunrise."

Check them out? I couldn't pronounce them. I wasn't entirely positive how to say "Maui."

Well, now I've seen a morsel of Hawaii—the outer crust of the former Sandwich Islands as it were—and I'm a believer. White sand beaches, swaying palm trees, emerald valleys swirled in mist . . . If Walt Disney with his corral of artists was around to conjure up a Cinemascopic version of earthly Eden he'd probably come up with something close to Hawaii.

For frostbacks shivering through yet another Canadian winter the islands have special resonance. Mangos on the trees . . . mynahs on the balcony . . . friendly natives who speak English better than you do—all in *December*?

It's almost pornographic.

And there are wonders the average Canadian simply doesn't have the mental equipment to absorb on first contact. The banyan tree in the centre of the town of Lahaina—a tree with multiple trunks and a canopy that covers as much terrain as Toronto's city hall. The sight of molten lava and snowdrifts. Both dripping down the same mountainside. Or beholding those strange eruptions out on the ocean. Great geysers of water shooting into the air. What's that about—underwater volcanoes? Incoming meteors? US navy war games?

Nope. Humpbacks. Whales as big as city buses and as homely as warty, waterlogged turnips. Blue-grey behemoths with ungainly pectoral fins protruding improbably like windmill blades from both sides of their heads, each fin a third of the beast's body length. Elfin-eyed and fulsomely be-barnacled, rocketing out of the water like gigantic, vulcanized Halloween creatures—breaching, flipper-slapping and generally acting like bumptious teenage boys on a testosterone overload.

Which in a sense they are. It's the male humpbacks that put on the show to wow the cows (and to cow other bulls). Each winter humpbacks come by the thousands, quite literally from the ends of the earth (they spend the rest of the year feeding in the frigid but food-rich waters of the northern and southern oceans) to make little humpbacks off Hawaii.

They are awesome, in the pre-Paris Hilton sense of the word—and quite undaunted by the presence of human voyeurs.

Mighty generous of them, considering we humans did our level best to wipe them out.

Whalers slaughtered over a quarter of a million humpbacks in the first half of the last century alone. By the time a moratorium was adopted in 1966 there were only a few thousand left in the world.

But they bounced back. And they bounce irrepressibly about the Hawaiian waters today, vaulting and crashing, thrusting their jaws, waving their flukes, occasionally flipping a two-storey pectoral into the sky in what looks like a giant "finger" to onlookers. It is impossible to feel anything less than elation, watching humpbacks. Tourists spontaneously cheer and applaud and weep with joy. You can't help yourself. "Most gamesome and light-hearted of all the whales," Melville said of them in *Moby Dick*. Feeling depressed? Go watch the humpbacks. You'll throw away your Prozac.

But these are big fellas. And they're horny. Any danger to onlookers? Nah. Humpbacks are fifty-tonne couch pillows as far as humans are concerned. They couldn't bite you if they wanted to—no teeth. They suck in their food—krill and tiny fish—through "baleen": boney plates in their jaws. Even though it's the size of a subway car, the humpback prefers the salad bar.

Why, it probably wouldn't even try to eat a humuhumunukunu-kuapua'a.

Who he? The state fish of Hawaii. Lives in reefs, looks like a Picasso painting with fins and is all of about twenty centimetres from nose to tail. The name is longer than the fish.

Hawaiian Islands? Should be called the Surprisin' Islands.

THE LOST LUGGAGE WARS

Revenge is a dish best eaten cold.

—OLD FRENCH PROVERB

Dave Carroll is the only civilian I know who ever won a battle in the Lost Luggage Wars.

Dave's a Nova Scotia musician who logs a lot of air miles travelling with his band, The Sons of Maxwell. Naturally, his guitar goes along for the ride. His custom-made Taylor acoustic travels in the hold, protected by a supposedly shock-proof case that is plastered with FRAGILE and DO NOT DROP stickers. Nonetheless, on a trip to Nebraska recently, United Airlines baggage handlers found a way to mangle the hell out of it. It cost Carroll $1,400 to repair the damage.

But when he approached United for compensation, the company stalled, blustered and eventually told him to get lost.

Dave Carroll didn't go postal, nor did he get suicidal. He got even.

Dave Carroll wrote a song.

The three-part ditty is entitled "United Breaks Guitars." You can see Dave perform the song on YouTube, if you care to.

You will be, as I type these words, approximately the twelve millionth visitor to do so. United's mugging of Dave's guitar, along with the company's "Tough luck, Bub" reaction turned into a musical goldmine for Dave Carroll and a public relations disaster for the airline. The massive public response to Dave's ditty led United to eventually offer a raft of flight vouchers as well as payment for the guitar repairs. Carroll shrewdly suggested that United donate the money to charity instead.

Final score: Dave Carroll, one; United Airlines, zilch.

Most of us don't fare nearly as well in the Lost Luggage Wars—my pal, Ms. D, for instance. This winter she landed in Mexico for a few weeks' vacation.

Her luggage, alas, kept flying.

All the way to Australia as it turned out—although it took her several days to discover that.

Well, what do you expect—Mexico, right? I asked her how bad it was, dealing with Mexican officialdom.

"The Mexicans were most helpful and business-like," Ms. D told me. "It was Air Canada that was absolutely hopeless." She talked to an AC rep who actually said, "I am not the brightest fruit on the tree, but I'll see what I can do." She asked to speak to his supervisor. She was told he was away until the following Monday. Eight days later her bags showed up.

Could have been worse, I suppose. She could have been Marie MacLaughlin. Air Canada managed to lose Marie's luggage for five days on a routine trip to Florida in December of 2008. On her return to Canada on Christmas Eve, the airline lost her bags *again*. In mid-January 2009 the airline's tracking system was still reporting that delivery of her luggage was being "initiated."

Which was interesting news for Marie. Her son had driven to the airport, hunted down and picked up the bags in person two weeks earlier.

This was after he'd tried for several days to get satisfaction through Air Canada's toll-free lost luggage number. "They were saying that the bag was at the airport but they couldn't confirm it, because they couldn't talk to anyone at the airport." The disconnect may be not unrelated to the fact that the toll-free number is connected to a call centre in India, some distance from the baggage carousels at Pearson International.

The lesson Marie MacLaughlin has taken from the fiasco? Avoid Air Canada. "I will probably never fly on them again," Marie says.

She'd better think twice about switching her business to United. A couple of months ago, Dave Carroll took a United Airlines flight to a gig in Denver, Colorado. Dave's no fool—he booked two seats on the flight—one for his guitar.

But his luggage? You guessed it—AWOL. It went on to Calgary and Fort Worth, Texas, before he saw it again.

Woody Allen couldn't make this stuff up.

TOO WEIRD FOR WORDS

Laughter: an orgasm triggered by the intercourse of reason with unreason.

— JACK KROLL

You know what makes me . . . ahem, laugh? The intrinsic absurdity of life on this whacky ball of dirt that's winging its way through the celestial void. Specifically, the way the human animal finds ingenious ways to make sure that the sublime is regularly cross-checked by the ridiculous.

Canada is particularly adept at this game. We gave the world:

Marshall McLuhan . . . and Don Cherry.

Ben Hepner . . . and Stompin' Tom Connors.

Pierre Trudeau . . . and Ralph Klein.

Professional hockey . . . and the Toronto Maple Leafs.

But there's an even finer example of loony juxtaposition that unfolded in the Great White North recently. And I mean the *real* Great White North—in the Arctic wastes between Greenland and Siberia. That's where you'll find the Gakkel Ridge.

What's that? It's an underwater mountain range. A great spine of rock sixteen thousand feet under the waves that runs along the ocean floor for over a thousand miles. Scientists are hot for the Gakkel Ridge because it too is hot—volcanic, in fact.

Undersea volcanoes often create hydrothermal vents—chimneys that spew superheated water into the surrounding ocean. Sometimes this leads to rare and exotic life forms found nowhere else in nature.

Long story short, an international expedition of icebreakers, support ships, robot amphibious submarines and antsy scientists eager to see what, if anything, is living down there began steaming toward the Gakkel Ridge last Canada Day. They expected to spend at least a month and a half on site.

Who—aside from the aforementioned boffins—cares? NASA, for one. Space Agency experts figure that techniques for operating robot vehicles under three miles of Arctic ocean could apply in the exploration of remote, frigid planets in outer space.

Okay, so where's the promised absurdity? That would be provided by Mr. Brooks Agnew, a physicist and futurist who lives in Kentucky. Mr. Agnew enlisted adventurers to accompany him on his own polar odyssey—the North Pole Inner Earth Expedition he called it—specifically to a spot precisely located at 84.4 degrees north and 41 degrees east, which is about, oh . . . 250 miles off the coast of Ellesmere Island.

That's where Mr. Agnew expected to find a portal leading to the centre of the earth—not to mention a previously unknown civilization. Planet Earth is really hollow, you see. And there are these two gateways—one near the North Pole and the other near the South Pole—that lead directly to the centre of the earth. "Everest has been climbed a hundred times," says Mr. Agnew. "The *Titanic* has been scanned from stem to stern. This is the first and only expedition to the North Pole opening ever attempted."

Er . . . quite.

Some of the people who accompanied Mr. Agnew firmly believe that our hollow planet is inhabited by the Lost Tribes of Israel who have mastered the art of living for hundreds of years and who protect their hidden world with fleets of flying saucers. Others are quite certain that the earth's core is the domain of a race of saurian aliens who hail from Venus.

Intrigued? If you had twenty grand burning a hole in your mattress you could have signed on with Mr. Agnew and joined him on his rented Russian icebreaker, the *Yamal*. You'd have sailed out of Murmansk last spring.

Originally, the North Pole Inner Earth Expedition was scheduled to set sail the very same week that the team of international scientists set off on their trek to investigate the Gakkel Ridge.

Who'da thunk it could come to this—a public firestorm over toilet paper? It's pretty hard to wax philosophic about something so mundane, but Andy Rooney gave it a shot. "I've noticed that Life is a lot like a roll of toilet paper," the *60 Minutes* gnome once said. "The closer you get to the end of it, the faster it goes."

That's not bad, but my sweetie has a riddle that's better:

How many men does it take to change a roll of toilet paper?

Nobody knows—it's never happened.

PUFF, PUFF AND AWAAAAAAY!

These be trying times for the nicotine-addicted among us, friends. Every day it seems there's a new list of places whence smokers are proscribed from indulging their vice. Lighting up is increasingly *verboten* in Canada's pubs and restaurants, in hotel lobbies and barbershops. Puffers have been ousted, coughing with outrage, from bus terminal waiting rooms, hockey arenas—even from the venerable Royal Canadian Legion, once famous for the penumbra of first-, second- and third-hand smoke it perpetually bathed in.

Some firms now forbid their employees to smoke in the company parking lot—even in the smokers' own cars. There's a community in California that has even banned smoking anywhere—including *out of doors.*

Hounded unmercifully from pillar to post and from ashtray to potted plant, what are smokers to do? Where can they go?

Simple. Go on-line. Google www.smintair.com and book a flight. Water the geraniums, get Aunt Edna to look after the cat, cancel the newspaper, pack your bags and take a cab to the airport. Check your bags, find your gate, climb aboard and smoke your brains out.

Smintair—it's a corporate contraction of Smoker's International Airways—not only lets you smoke in flight, it *wants* you to. Cigarettes, cigars, pipe or hookah. Black tobacco, blonde tobacco or Burmese coarse leaf. Matinee Lites or Turkish Ovals. Smoke 'em if you got 'em.

Smintair is the brainchild of Alexander Schoppmann, a

middle-aged German entrepreneur who wants the world to return to what he recalls as the glory days of commercial flying. That would be pre-1990s, before airlines throughout Europe and North America imposed smoking bans on all their flights.

Herr Schoppmann remembers a golden—well, yellowish-brown—age before that. An age when, as the lumbering North Stars and DC-8s feathered their way across the skies, beautiful, smiling stewardesses served delicious meals on snow-white linen with real silverware.

And when the meal was done and you settled back with a brandy or a Spanish coffee, here came the stewardess *to light your cigar.*

"The whole bloody plane was a party," recalls Schoppmann. "It was great."

And Schoppmann intends for it to be great once more. Starting in March of next year, Schoppmann hopes to have two heavily modified Boeing 747s in daily service. Instead of shoe-horning 500 passengers aboard, Schoppmann's birds will accommodate just 138—30 in first class, 108 in business.

On Smintair, nobody travels steerage ("Hospitality Class" in Air Canada Newspeak).

What's more there will be first-class dining for all. Menus featuring French, Italian, Chinese and Japanese cuisine, not to mention a lounge on the upper deck, at least three open bars, luxurious sofas, a duty-free shop, a recreation centre, a two-hundred-movie entertainment database and best of all, actual leg-room fit for Kareem Abdul Jabarr in every single seat—six point seven feet's worth if you're flying first class.

Which brings us to the bad news.

The price.

It ain't gonna be cheap to fly Smintair. You'll pay $9,300 for a return ticket flying business. That rises to a stratospheric $14,350 for a single first-class return.

Which brings us to the second piece of bad news.

In order to avail yourself of Smintair's invitation to smoke your brains out at 35,000 feet, you're first going to have to make your way to, um . . .

Germany.

Or Japan.

That's the only route Smintair's nailed down so far—daily flights between Düsseldorf and Tokyo's Narita airport. So you can tack on another few thousand bucks just to get from Canada to there and back.

Nine thousand . . . fifteen thousand . . . we're looking at pretty close to twenty thousand bucks here.

Maybe it really is time to quit.

GOODIES FROM ON HIGH

There are more strange things in heaven and earth,
Horatio, than are dreamed of in your philosophy.

Indeed there are, Hamlet my son. New Brunswick's Reversing Falls and the existence of Sarah Palin as an elective option spring to mind. But worldly weirdness is not limited to Saint John and Wasilla, Alaska. We also have John From and cargo cults.

Or perhaps it's Jon From. Or John Frum. Nobody's quite sure because nobody, aside from a few thousand natives in the South Pacific, thinks there ever was a John From.

Nonetheless, countless natives believe. In Vanuatu, each February 15, followers celebrate John From Day. And John From disciples are certain that one day their leader will appear and bestow upon the Faithful all the goodies—TV sets, stereos, matching Hummers—that us white folks have been jealously hoarding all these years.

The John From phenomenon first appeared more than half a century ago during World War II, when American troops swarmed into the South Pacific theatre. Upwards of 300,000 GIs were airlifted into what was then called the New Hebrides. Natives of the islands had never seen such an awesome display of power, wealth and splendour. They were also gobsmacked by the down-home friendliness of these Gods From on High. Imagine—divine creatures that approached you with open arms, friendly smiles and greetings like "Howdy, I'm John from Wyoming," and "Hi, I'm John from Kentucky."

The New Hebrideans didn't know Kentucky from Wyoming

from Kangerlussuaq, Greenland, but they heard the greeting "Hi, I'm John from . . ." often enough to conclude that they were meeting a deity who answered to the name "John From."

Or Jon Frum—the spelling didn't matter. To the natives John From was an ethereal amalgam of Uncle Sam, Santa Claus and the Tooth Fairy. They just knew that if they were good little Fromians, they would one day be rewarded with immense wealth. What kind of wealth? Cargo wealth. And where would this wealth come from? The same place all those friendly GIs came from—the bellies of the giant iron birds that roared across their skies.

Mind you, the New Hebrideans were kind of an easy audience. They had already been rolled over by platoons of fire-and-brimstone Christian missionaries who came out to civilize the heathen and to acquaint them with their innate sinfulness.

And to get some clothes on those women, for mercy's sake.

As a matter of fact, some anthropologists speculate that John From and the cargo cult evolved in reaction to all those grim and joyless Bible-thumpers. John From advocated singing, dancing and drinking. No wonder he looked good. In 1941 John From disciples rose up, albeit non-violently. They left the mission schools and churches, abandoned the plantations where they'd been put to work and retreated to the interior, where they established new villages and attempted to resurrect their ancient rituals, feasts and dances.

They proceeded to try and call down heavenly blessings from John From. They built symbolic landing strips deep in the jungle, based on what they'd seen at US Air Force bases. They laid coloured strips of cloth in the trees and constructed thatch hut approximations of airport buildings and hangars.

And waited for manna to rain down on them.

Some of them are still waiting. The John From Movement has been around for more than fifty years now. Do they still expect to actually see John From one day? Absolutely. "He is our God, our Jesus," Chief Isaak Wan Nikiau told a BBC interviewer. "One day he will return."

Well—primitives, eh? What do you expect? These people are barely out of the Stone Age. They're not sophisticated like you. And me. And the guy who wrote this about religious intolerance:

Imagine a world in which generations of human beings came to believe that certain films were made by God or that specific software was coded by Him.

Imagine a future in which millions of our descendants murder each other over rival interpretations of *Star Wars* or Windows 98.

Author Sam Harris wrote that a few years back in his book *Letter to a Christian Nation*. Then he added the obvious: we don't have to imagine the above scenario.

We're living it, pal.

TREE'S COMPANY

*No one has ever successfully painted or photographed
a redwood tree. The feeling they produce is not
transferable. From them comes silence and awe. It's
not only their unbelievable stature, nor the color which
seems to shift and vary under your eyes, no, they are
not like any trees we know. They are ambassadors from
another time.*

—JOHN STEINBECK, *TRAVELS WITH CHARLEY*

Once you've seen one redwood, you've seen them all.

—RONALD REAGAN

Different strokes, I guess. John Steinbeck was an artist, with a
writer's eye and a writer's sensibility. Ronald Reagan was . . .
not. Even his staunchest supporters never pretended that the Gipper
was any kind of mental giant. It was Reagan, after all, who once
assured reporters that trees *caused* pollution.

I wish I could weigh in on the subject of the giant California redwood's magnificence or lack thereof, but the fact is I have never seen
a specimen first-hand.

I've seen plenty of mighty fine trees, mind, from colour-besotted
sugar maples in the Eastern Townships of Quebec to otherworldly
red cedars looming Emily Carrishly out of the rainforests of BC.
There's a knobby old apple tree with my initials carved in it growing out of a hillside in southern Ontario, and I still have a diamond

willow walking stick I plucked as a branch from a thicket on the outskirts of Whitehorse in the Yukon.

Joyce Kilmer famously wrote:

I think that I shall never see
A poem lovely as a tree.

I agree with him. I have luscious memories of strolling under arbutus and beech and Garry oak and pines that I wouldn't trade for any number of Pindaric odes or Petrarchan sonnets. And I still remember marvelling at a stunted stand of gnarled and twisted black spruce leaning away from an Atlantic gale on the Newfoundland coast.

We live in a land that's sky high in magnificent timber, but I had to leave Canada and travel nearly five thousand kilometres to the west, to a volcanic outcrop of the Hawaiian Islands, to look up into the most incredible tree I've ever seen.

It stands, improbably enough, smack in the middle of the town of Lahaina on the island of Maui. The tree—*Ficus bengalensis*—is precisely 137 years old. We know that because the history books tell us that the sheriff of Maui, one William O. Smith, planted an eight-foot banyan sapling, lately arrived from India, in the Lahaina courthouse square on April 24, 1873. Lahaina at the time was still smarting over its demotion from capital city and royal seat of the islands. King Kamehameha III, Hawaii's last reigning monarch, had moved his royal court to Honolulu, leaving Lahaina to fend for itself as a roughhouse whaling port and depot for the sugar cane industry. Today, Lahaina is primarily a tourist town whose main exports are T-shirts, snorkel excursions and heftily priced tickets to luau extravaganzas.

Lahaina's banyan hasn't grown all that tall in its thirteen decades under the broiling Hawaiian sun—it's only about fifty feet high at the crown.

It's the horizontal spread of the tree that astounds.

First-time viewers often think they have entered a banyan forest. The best part of an acre—way more than a city block—is shaded by a dense, three-storey-high mat of leaves that towers over some seventeen massive tree trunks looming up from the courtyard. Only one of them is the true trunk. The others grew from aerial roots that dropped over the years from the tree canopy to the ground below.

The banyan tree is Lahaina's town square, piazza, village common and local gathering place all rolled into one. There's room under its boughs for over a thousand people to shelter from the blistering sun or the infrequent rains. Each December it becomes the world's largest Christmas tree as thousands of lights are strung from its branches.

But the Lahaina banyan's greatest performance occurs each evening just as the sun goes down.

The tree *erupts* in an ear-shattering cacophony of screeching and cawing.

Mynah birds. Thousands of them returning to the tree to roost for the night, just as they have for generations. The noise they make is unearthly. And magnificent.

At the risk of paraphrasing Joyce Kilmer:

I think that I shall never hear
A poem lovely as a tree.

PART TWO

CULTURE IS FOR YOGURT

HOW TO STIRRUP
THE ART WORLD

Emerging artist alert: have you seen the paintings of Cholla? Abstracts, primarily. Watercolours for the most part.

Stunning. I'm no expert on the visual arts, but it seems to me Cholla's canvases positively resonate with glimmers of A.Y. Jackson and Lawren Harris.

But don't take my word for it—ask John Yimin. He *is* an expert. He's a California art lover and an art critic—and he's absolutely smitten with the works of the painting phenomenon. "The brush strokes Cholla uses to get his vision down on paper," writes Yimin, "the watercolours' dance . . . and especially the fascinating completion of the works . . . grabs me and holds me with the fire of Pollock and the fixed gaze of Resnick."

High praise for an artist who's only twenty-three years old, with decades of creativity stretching out before him like the Woodbine racetrack.

And Cholla appears to be embracing his destiny at full gallop. Already he's been a featured guest on Martha Stewart's television show. He's also had exhibitions in San Francisco and New York.

Best of all, for those of us who lack the deep pockets of major art collectors, Cholla's works are still fairly affordable. You can pick up some of his earlier works for as little as US$900. Even his best canvases seldom fetch more than $2500.

But my advice would be—hurry. Cholla's got a landscape called *The Big Red Buck* that will soon be featured in an art show called Arte Laguna in Mogliano Veneto, Italy. Once his work gets international recognition his prices are bound to go supernova.

Yep. Major shows in US galleries. National exposure on television. An upcoming gig at one of the most prestigious art exhibitions in Europe.

Not bad. For a horse.

Yes, Cholla is of the equine persuasion. A copper-coloured buckskin mustang–quarterhorse cross, born on a Nevada ranch in 1985. Cholla might have spent his life rounding up confused little dogies and absent-minded cows had not his owner, an amateur artist, noticed that he loved to pick up things with his teeth. On a whim, she tacked a piece of paper on a corral post, stroked a paint-laden artist's paintbrush across it and held the brush out to Cholla.

The rest was Art History 101.

Cholla graduated to an industrial-strength easel that stands in his corral. Nobody rotates the paper or manipulates the easel. Cholla chomps down on the brush and paints what he likes.

But is it Art?

His customers certainly think so. So does Kurt Kohl, an art curator based in McLean, Virginia. "(Cholla) is creating art on the level of a young child," says Kohl. "There may not be a lot of thought behind the process, but one could ask the same question about Pollock or De Kooning or Rothko."

Indeed. Or about Jan Fabre, Subodh Gupta and Jeff Koons. Gupta gave us the mammoth skull made out of ice buckets that sits outside the Palazzo Grassi in Venice. We can be grateful to Jan Fabre for the giant bug impaled on a seven-foot high steel needle in Leuven, Belgium.

And who can forget Jeff Koons's seminal work, *Three Ball 50/50 Tank*, which, last I heard, was still enthralling audiences at the Museum of Modern Art in Manhattan? It consists of three basketballs floating in a half-filled glass tank of distilled water.

Philistine? Moi? Well, maybe just a little. Seems to me that if Art was a game of tennis, the lads could be accused of playing with the net down. But what do I know? Art's flickering standards have long been a source of deep confusion to me.

Take the case of *Newport Nude*, a painting by Sir Gerald Kelly, which was bought by a public gallery in England in 1947 but then removed from public view and locked in a vault on the grounds that the woman portrayed in the painting was . . . well, *nude*. Very nude, if you catch my drift. Indecent and whatnot. This past summer, what with our new relaxed standards and all, *Newport Nude* was reinstated in the public gallery.

Alas, the authorities have seen fit to ban the painting once more. Not because the model is full-frontal nude. No problem with that.

But she has . . . a lit cigarette in her hand.

If Cholla could read this, you know what kind of a laugh he'd be having.

THE WORST WRITER
OF ALL TIME

Never heard of Amanda McKittrick Ros? Count your blessings.

Ms. Ros was an Irish lass who was born in 1860. The name on her birth certificate reads Amanda Malvina Fitzalan Anna Margaret McLelland McKittrick, and that should have been a clue right there, for anyone who comes into the world so encumbered and shackled by vowels and consonants is bound to have issues with the English language. And she did. Ms. Ros became a writer.

Many believe she became the very worst writer in the English-speaking world.

She produced three novels and several volumes of verse, all of them howlingly bad. Here, for instance, is a passage from her novel *Irene Iddesleigh*:

"Leave me now, deceptive demons of deluded mockery; lurk no more around the vale of vanity, like a vindictive viper, strike the lyre of living deception to the strains of dull deadness, despair and doubt."

Ms. Ros lived to the age of ninety-nine, blissfully certain to the end that she was a great writer. She imagined her reading audience as "the million and one who thirst for aught that drops from my pen."

She was pretty bad, but there's no reason for Canadians to shuffle shamelessly, toque in hand, when it comes to bad writers. After all, we have James McIntyre.

McIntyre came to Canada from Scotland as a child in 1841 and eventually settled in the town of Ingersoll, in the heart of southern Ontario dairy country.

James McIntyre and dairy cows: a marriage made in poetry heaven.

McIntyre became known as the Cheese Poet. He had verses for every occasion—providing the occasion involved cheesemaking. His verses offered advice:

Our Muse it doth refuse to sing
Of cheese made early in the spring,
When cows give milk from spring fodder
You cannot make a good cheddar.

Fodder, cheddar. Sure, that . . . almost rhymes.

McIntyre's masterpiece? Well, it's hard to beat his "Ode on the Mammoth Cheese Weighing Over 7,000 Pounds." This is a poem written about an actual, three-and-a-half-tonne cheese that was produced as a PR stunt in Ingersoll in 1866.

We have seen thee, Queen of Cheese
Lying quietly at your ease,
Gently fanned by evening breeze;
Thy fair form no flies dare seize.

The famous Ingersoll cheese was slated to go on exhibition in Toronto, New York and Great Britain, but McIntyre envisaged even grander travels:

May you not receive a scar as
We have heard that Mr. Harris
Intends to send you off as far as
The great World's Show at Paris.

James McIntyre didn't write just about cheese. He was a versatile artist, more than capable of turning his creative talents to other subjects, like, well, sweet corn:

For it doth make best ensilage
For those in dairying engage
It makes the milk in streams to flow,
Where dairymen have a good silo.

So in the end, who's the worst—McIntyre or Ros? Well, I'd love to be a homer, but I'm afraid the Irish wordmonger deserves first place. Hard to top her last novel, *Helen Huddleson*, in which the characters are all named after fruits—Lord Raspberry, Sir Peter Plum and the Earl of Grape—and how do you top this description of "Madame Pear" and her "swell staff of sweet-faced helpers swathed stratagem, whose members and garments glowed with the lust of the loose, sparkled with the tears of the tortured, shone with the sunlight of bribery, dangled with the diamonds of distrust, slashed with the sapphires of scandals" and, well, it goes on. Sorry, but even Canada's Cheese Poet can't compete with talent like that.

Not that Amanda Ros would have doubted her supremacy for a moment. "I expect I will be talked about at the end of a thousand years," she once said.

I fear she might be right.

KANYE JUDGE A BOOK
BY ITS COVER?

"Who's Kanye West?" I asked my son. He looked at me like I'd just tumbled off the back of a turnip truck from Sheep Tracks, Alberta. "You're kidding, right?" he responded.

I wasn't kidding. I'd never heard of the guy until I read the story in the newspaper about his new book.

So I Googled him. Turns out Kanye West is famous. A pop music star, born in Chicago in 1978 and currently a household name (not counting my household) around the world as a rapper, record producer and hip hop phenom.

What can I tell you—I'm an old fart. I know as many nuclear physicists as I do hip-hoppers—and I don't know any nuclear physicists.

But I found out about Kanye when he swam into my ken, if you will. The guy's authored a book called *Thank You And You're Welcome*. It's described as his "personal philosophy."

It is fifty-two pages long.

What's more, some of the pages are blank; others are just sprinkled with a handful of words.

Like the page that carries the sentence: "I HATE THE WORD HATE!"

Or the two-page spread that informs readers: "LIFE IS FIVE

PERCENT WHAT HAPPENS AND 95 PERCENT HOW YOU REACT!"

My, that's original. I haven't heard that bromide since my Boy Scout troop leader laid it on us during a wienie roast at Camp Calumet about half a century ago.

Call me a cynic, but fifty-two pages of blank space interspersed with recycled clichés strikes me as a tad effervescent as philosophical treatises go. Deep sledding for Kanye though—so much so that he had a co-author, one J. Sakiya Sandifer, to help him slog through the really heavy stuff.

Seems as if the whole world of books and writing is deeply distasteful to Kanye. Even though he condescended to take questions from reporters about his new book, he clearly wasn't keen about it.

"I am not a fan of books," he said. "I would never want a book's autograph."

Probably just as well. It's hard to find a book with legible handwriting skills.

Kanye went on to tell reporters he was "a proud non-reader of books. I like to get information from doing stuff like actually talking to people and living real life."

Google informs me that Kanye got a pretty gritty slice of real life at the MTV Awards awhile back. He was nominated in five different categories including Best Male Artist. He whiffed in every category.

And did not take it well. Kanye had a five-alarm hissy fit right in front of the cameras. Shook his fist, stamped up and down, laid down a cluster of F-bombs, denounced the judges and the competition and declared that he would "not come back to MTV ever again."

If Kanye ever does change his mind about reading he might find it profitable to glance through a chapter or two by Emily Post. She had some helpful things to say about public etiquette.

Probably never happen. There is a thread of anti-egghead defiance that runs through Kanye's published work. His first album was called *Dropout*. The next one was *Late Registration*, followed by *Graduation*.

Which Kanye didn't—he's a college flunkee and proud of it. He claims being a non-reader of other authors was helpful in "writing" his book because it gave him "a childlike purity."

I prefer another entertainer's take on books. Walt Disney said:

"There is more treasure in books than in all the pirates' loot on Treasure Island . . . and best of all, you can enjoy these riches every day of your life."

I also like what a chap named Gilbert Highet had to say when a visitor dismissed his collection of "mere books." Highet retorted, "These are not books, lumps of lifeless paper, but *minds* alive on the shelves. From each of them goes out its own voice . . . and just as the touch of a button on our set will fill the room with music, so by taking down one of these volumes and opening it, one can call into range the voice of a man far distant in time and space, and hear him speaking to us, mind to mind, heart to heart."

Amen, Gilbert. Kanye dig it, Kanye?

TAKE THIS NAME AND CHEV IT

The aquarium is gone. Everywhere, giant, finned cars
nose forward like fish;
a savage servility slides by on grease.
—ROBERT LOWELL

There is the Stingray, of course. And the Marlin. And the Barracuda—though it isn't essential to have scales to be immortalized in steel. Horses do well too—Charger, Bronco, Pinto, Mustang. Birds are also fully represented: Blackhawk, Falcon, Thunderbird and Lark. Even insects—Wasp, Scarab, Hornet and Beetle—make the cut.

What do all these critters have in common? Well, they're all members of the animal kingdom, but they are also the names of cars. We love to name our vehicles after animals (I haven't even mentioned Impala, Jaguar, Cougar, Bobcat, Lynx, Rabbit, Ram and Fox). The reason for this long-time love affair may have been uncovered in a study conducted by researchers at the University of Vienna. The study suggests that subconsciously we think of cars as living creatures.

The researchers presented forty young adults—half male, half female—with photographs of the front ends of thirty-eight late-model automobiles, all the same colour. "What do you see?" the researchers asked. "A face," was the overwhelming answer.

More than 90 percent of the cars evoked a face for members of the study group. They considered the headlights to be "eyes" looking back at them. They regarded the radiator/grill to be a nose and mouth. Many of the cars had more than faces; they had Attitude. Some friendly; some not.

Sounds primitive and it probably is. You and I are only alive today because our ancestors were better than their neighbours at danger recognition. Our prehistoric forebears could "read" the facial expressions of strangers and other animals swiftly enough to decide whether they were friend or foe. The quick studies, like your kin and mine, survived. The slower ones? Sabre-toothed tiger bait.

Automakers picked up on this curious human tic a long time ago. That's why the front ends of so many cars look dominant, masculine, arrogant—even angry-looking. Stands to reason if we buy such a car, it's on our side, right?

Mind you, not every customer wants a macho marauder for personal transportation. Some drivers prefer friendly, submissive faces in their carport. Smart cars don't look tough or threatening. Neither do the Volkswagen Beetle, the Nissan Micra or the Kia Picanto.

But auto designers have to be very careful where they draw the line. A car can look cute, but not wussy. And you definitely don't want the front of a new car to put potential customers in mind of, um, bodily orifices.

You could ask the designers of the ill-fated Ford Edsel about that.

However we design them and whatever we name them, there's no question that the automobile profoundly influences the lives we lead as North Americans—for better and for worse. The US architect Philip Johnson pronounced the automobile "the greatest catastrophe in the entire history of city architecture." John Keats, the author and Kingston, Ontario, native, went even further. In his bestseller called *The Insolent Chariots* Keats wrote: "The automobile changed our dress, manners, social customs, vacation habits, the shape of our cities, consumer purchasing patterns, common tastes and positions in intercourse."

Oh—and don't forget causes of death. In the past fifty years more than 200,000 Canadians have died either at the wheel or under them. That's more than we lost in both world wars combined.

Anyway you slice it, the four-wheeled gas guzzlers rule. They define our cities and they endlessly criss-cross our rural spaces. They dictate where we live and work, they bloom like viruses in our public spaces and they attach themselves like barnacles to our expressways, streets and laneways. Someone asked the American historian and literary critic Lewis Mumford to nominate the national flower. "The concrete cloverleaf," he replied glumly.

Canada's own Joni Mitchell put it better: "They paved paradise and put up a parking lot."

THE CORN WAS AS HIGH . . .

Let's have some new clichés!

—SAMUEL GOLDWYN

O wayfaring strangers, cherished colleagues, friends and neighbours and, it goes without saying, my nearest and dearest. It warms the cockles of my heart to arrive at the realization that we are gathered here together for one common purpose on this day of all days. For truly it must be said that we find ourselves, citizens of a grateful nation, in a land of plenty, nevertheless poised on the brink of perilous yet challenging times. The torch has been passed, the gauntlet thrown down, the challenge issued.

To wit: what can be done about the cliché?

The truth is, it is hard *not* to write or speak in clichés, because clichés have one abiding asset: they are extremely apt—or at least they were when they were first born. And we find them everywhere. Look at how we plunder our fellow creatures to mine clichés. Virtually everything with fin, fur or feather has been usurped. We even double-down our clichés by turning them into cliché/similes. We can describe a fellow human as sleek as an otter or fat as a pig, dumb as an ox or sly as a weasel, eagle-eyed or blind as a bat. Humans can be turned into fish in a barrel, ducks in a row, birds on a wire or monkeys in the middle. We have wise owls, dumb bunnies, old trout and young bucks.

And a fly on the wall tells me that you, gentle reader, have at various times in your life been described as a dirty rat, a dog in the manger, a snake in the grass, a fox in the henhouse and a cat amongst the pigeons.

Even our moods are animalized. It is possible to be happy as (a) a clam (b) a sheep in clover or (c) a pig in . . . ah, but that's a horse of a different colour.

The problem with clichés? Shelf life. Some of the most lacklustre, dreary clichés in the language sprang from the quill pen of the best writer we ever had. He was a tower of strength who could have you in stitches, set your teeth on edge, leave you tongue-tied with knitted brow and bated breath. He could make you vanish into thin air or not budge an inch. He could render you white as the driven snow or dead as a doornail.

All of those expressions would earn you a groan from a high school English teacher, but they were, ahem, bright-eyed and bushy-tailed when William Shakespeare first coined them. It's not Shakespeare's fault they now sound trite. The Bard hasn't set pen to parchment for over four centuries yet we're still recycling his best stuff.

But clichés go back way beyond Shakespeare's time. A bird in the hand, an eye for an eye, a thorn in the flesh and a lamb to the slaughter—all come from the Bible.

And that old chestnut "bite the dust." Who first said that—a long-forgotten baseball umpire? Ronald Reagan playing a US marshal in some spaghetti western?

Not even close. Homer coined that phrase more than two millennia ago.

The most enthusiastic cliché spouters these days? Jocks, I think. There must be a school that hockey defencemen, football linebackers and basketball sharpshooters attend to learn phrases like: "We're gonna play them one game at a time"; "We gave a hunnert and ten percent"; and "We need a total team effort."

Clichés owe their existence to the simple fact that at one time, somewhere, they were perfect and brilliant and fresh. But, like chewing gum, clichés go flat through overuse. Then they become the refuge of the lazy, the brain-dead and politicians. (But I repeat myself.)

Politicians adore the cliché because it's safe—all voters put their brains on idle when they hear phrases like "bipartisan solution," "leadership by example" and "level playing field." The effect is hypnotic, not to mention stupefying—and it's a tactic that shows no sign of giving up the ghost, kicking the bucket, cashing in its chips or joining the choir invisible.

But the cliché is merely a wrung-out figure of speech. A dead metaphor, if you will. All any decent writer has to do is put his nose to the grindstone, roll up his sleeves, set his shoulder to the wheel, pull himself up by his bootstraps, fix his eye on the prize, keep a stiff upper lip, throw his back into it and resolve to stop using them entirely.

Now you know. Go and sin no more.

And metaphors be with you.

ADDICTED TO DICTIONARIES

Dictionaries are like watches; the worst is better than none, and the best cannot be expected to go quite true.
—SAMUEL JOHNSON

I've got at least seven dictionaries scattered around my house. I'm talking about general, A to Z, look-up-a-word dictionaries. I've also got a slew of arcane, so-called dictionaries on everything from Precambrian geology to conversational Hawaiian.

But those seven general word dictionaries are my babies. I've got the *Gage Canadian* and the *Random House Webster*; the *Coles Concise English* and the *Oxford Essential Desk Reference.* I've even got the granddaddy of all English dictionaries—the *Oxford Unabridged.* That's the one that comes in two hernia-inducing volumes crammed with type so fine you have to read it with a magnifying glass. Which is way too much trouble, even for a word freak like me. Betcha I haven't cracked my OED in five years.

I don't revere my dictionaries; I use them like a farmer uses baling wire. Dictionaries are my workbench, my toolbox, my potting shed. Not to mention my hard-core addiction. I'm with Alfred Jay Nock, who said: "As sheer casual reading matter, I still find the English dictionary the most interesting book in our language."

That said, there is one dictionary that will never come through my front door. It's called the *Oxford Junior Dictionary.* No loss—it was never intended for me anyway. It's aimed at children, aged seven or older. But if I was a parent—or teacher—of young children, I'd be very worried about that.

When the latest edition hit the bookstores, it caused a bit of a fuss. Not so much for what's between its covers, as for what's been left out.

You will not find the word "aisle" among the OJD's 10,000 entries. Nor will you find "altar," "vicar" or "minister." "Disciple" is missing, as is "pulpit" and "parish"; "monk" and "nun."

Why the anti-religious slant? Vineeta Gupta, the person in charge of children's dictionaries at Oxford University Press, explains: "Nowadays . . . we are much more multicultural. People don't go to church as often as before. Our understanding of religion is within multiculturalism, which is why some words such as 'Pentecost' or 'Whitsun' would have been in twenty years ago, but not now."

I suppose Pentecost and Whitsun are a little dated—but "bishop"? "Psalm"? "Carol"? "Saint"? "Devil"? You won't find those in the *Oxford Junior Dictionary* either.

Not that the book restricts itself to theological assaults. It's not fond of imperialism either. Thus, coronation, duchess, duke, emperor and monarch will not be found in its pages. Harry Potter fans won't be pleased. Neither "dwarf" nor "elf" nor "goblin" made the cut. And should an inquisitive child wish to know about mosses and ferns, said child will have to consult some source other than the *Oxford Junior Dictionary*. The book pretty much dismisses the natural world in favour of the Brave New one.

"When you look back at older versions of dictionaries," explains Ms. Gupta, "there were lots of examples of flowers . . . because many children lived in semi-rural environments and saw the seasons. Nowadays, the environment has changed."

Sure has if you go by the *Oxford Junior*. No buttercups in here, kiddies. Likewise no carnation, clover, dandelion, gooseberry or heather. The animal world is similarly decimated. No mention of beaver, goldfish, hamster, leopard, raven or wren.

The world-famous naturalist and painter, Robert Bateman, is appalled by the *Oxford Junior Dictionary*. "This is another nail in the coffin of human beings being acquainted with nature," he says.

Mind you, there are some words in the *Oxford Junior Dictionary* that are missing from my tomes. "Blog" is in the book. So are "voice mail," "database," and "MP3 player."

But really—at the expense of losing words like "violet" and "willow"? No more "pelican" or "porcupine"? "We are looking at the loss of words of great beauty," says Anthony Seldon, headmaster of Wellington College in Berkshire. "I would rather have 'marzipan' and 'mistletoe' than 'MP3 player.'"

Of all my dictionaries, the one I use most is *Webster's Third International*. My copy is huge—it's also old. I rescued it from the Metro Toronto Library discard bin back in the late 1960s. And it contains about 465,000 more words than the *Oxford Junior Dictionary*—several thousand of which I have yet to savour.

No mention of "MP3 player" in its 2,263 pages.

But you should read the entry for "marzipan."

SOUNDING OFF ABOUT NOISE

*There is something terribly wrong with a culture
inebriated by noise.*

—GEORGE STEINER

Noise is to music as weeds are to flowers. We encourage the latter and do our damnedest to stomp the former out of our lives. That said, there's a lot more noise than music in our lives these days. Just think of some of the day-to-day sounds we take for granted that would utterly mystify our forebears. My grandparents never had their innards massaged by a throbbing in-car stereo. They never heard a nail gun. They wouldn't know what to make of the beep of a microwave oven or that eerie four-bar flourish that announces the arrival of Microsoft Windows on our computers.

My grandparents never suffered the roar of a snowmobile or a leaf blower at full throttle—and they certainly never heard an LRAD.

Neither, for that matter, have I—and I don't want to.

LRAD stands for Long-range Acoustic Device. Military types with their charming gift for euphemism—they're the folks who dubbed flesh-shredding land mines "anti-personnel devices"—have outdone themselves with their description of the LRAD. They call it "a communication device." More accurately, it is a "sound cannon"— a weapon that can blow you right out of your socks.

The LRAD is basically a loudspeaker on steroids. It can be (and has been) employed by law enforcement officers to disperse protesters, rioters or . . . well, anybody that the authorities find annoying but not worth killing outright. When the trigger is pulled on the LRAD cannon, anyone it's aimed at will be assaulted by an ululating siren-like screech that can be precisely, and painfully, calibrated.

How loud is an LRAD blast? Sticking your head next to a stage amp at a Rolling Stones concert might subject you to 120 decibels. At 130 dB you'd be writhing on the ground. At 140 dB your hearing deteriorates and you experience permanent hearing loss. The LRAD can deliver an aural punch up to 152 dB.

Some communication device.

Sound as a weapon. Just what we need in a world of chainsaws, car alarms and ambulance sirens.

There should be an upside to living in increasingly noisier times. You'd think that we'd be getting fussier and more discriminating in the noise department. You'd hope that the back-alley beating we've been giving our ears would at least make us appreciate the subtleties of *nice* noise, i.e., music. Sadly, the opposite appears to be the case. The sound quality that comes out of a standard compact disc is infinitely superior to the sound that emanates from those dinky MP3 players. But compact disc players, alas, aren't all that compact compared to an MP3 player, which allows a listener to tote around up to four thousand tunes on his hip. Accordingly, CDs are on the wane and every third person you meet is walking around with tiny noise-channelling amplifiers embedded in their earholes—even though the sound is decidedly inferior, even crummy.

As a matter of fact, a music professor at Stanford University claims he has evidence that younger listeners actually prefer what he calls "lo-fi" versions of popular songs to hi-fi ones. He claims that to a large percentage of the new generation, popular music is *supposed* to sound muddy and indistinct. More noise in our lives—and this time it's entirely self-inflicted.

But some might argue it's not noisy enough out there. Take hybrid cars. The knock on hybrids is that they're *too* quiet. Cyclists and pedestrians can't hear them coming the way they can hear old gas-burning, piston-chugging ordinary cars and trucks. Collisions between hybrids and cyclists or pedestrians are way up.

Automobile manufacturers are now searching for some kind of aural warning device that can be attached to hybrids to let people know there's an electric vehicle bearing down on them—but what kind of sound? A honk? A whistle? A three-bar yodel from Lyle Lovett?

Whatever the final solution, you can bet your hearing aid it'll be yet another noise your grandparents never had to put up with.

DINOSAURS ROCK ON!

*Rock music is the most brutal, ugly, vicious form of
expression . . . sly, lewd—in plain fact, dirty . . . a
rancid-smelling aphrodisiac . . . martial music of every
delinquent on the face of the earth.*
—FRANK SINATRA, 1957

Yeah, right. This, from Old Blue Eyes, a guy who partied with
mobsters, smacked hookers around and had people he didn't
care for beaten up by hired thugs. But he loathed rock 'n' roll. Just
like Pierre Berton.

Berton? The savviest Canuck ever to peck out a newspaper column. Back in the 1960s, he wrote for the *Toronto Daily Star* five days
a week and he did it for many years. His turf was the right-hand edge
of the second section, and he used his space to churn out exposes,
satires, profiles, rants and raves. His research was breathtaking, his
wit was biting and, more than a few times, his gall was unmitigated.

Berton was, in the old untrivialized sense of the word, awesome.
But he wasn't perfect. Each December he produced a column of year-
end predictions, and in it, he invariably announced with unshakeable
confidence that the musical times, they were a-changin'. Rock 'n' roll,
he assured his readers, was finally on its deathbed.

He was wrong. It's a half-century later and rock 'n' roll still isn't
extinct—whereas Pierre Berton is. As a matter of fact, some of the
rock groups that most outraged Berton and Sinatra half a century ago
are still on the circuit.

Hang around Vancouver's GM Place, or Toronto's Air Canada Centre and sooner or later a scalper will offer you tickets for the latest incarnation of the Kinks, the Who, the Hollies, the Troggs . . .

And of course . . . the Stones.

The Rolling Stones. What a force of nature is there, my friends. Mick and the boys have been enthralling kids and infuriating parents since nineteen-sixty-freaking-two, if you can believe it. And that's despite people trying to bury them from the beginning.

Forty years ago Truman Capote looked at Jagger and sniffed: "He moves like a parody between a majorette girl and Fred Astaire."

In 1971 John Lennon said: "I think it's a lot of hype. I like 'Honky Tonk Woman' but I think Mick's a joke, with all that fag dancing; I always did. I enjoy it, I'll probably go and see his films and all, like everybody else, but really, I think it's a joke."

Yeah, well. Time has passed. Jagger's still strutting and prancing while Capote and Lennon are playing in some underworld backup band with Old Blue Eyes.

And Pierre Berton's doing PR for them.

Who could've imagined it? Not Marianne Faithfull, that's for sure. Way back in the early sixties, the English rock star was already writing off the Stones:

"You can't go on doing that thing for years. I mean, just imagine having to sing 'Satisfaction' when you're forty-five."

Jagger is still singing about his lack of satisfaction—and he hasn't seen forty-five for better than two decades.

Of course, nobody's harder on old rock 'n' rollers than old rock 'n' rollers themselves. Remember loveable, winsome, self-deprecating flower child Joni Mitchell? So does David Crosby, who played with her (in all senses of the word) back in the sixties. "Joni," recalls Crosby, "was about as modest as Mussolini."

Grace Slick was no kinder to her bandmate Paul Kantner, a man not renowned for his linguistic smarts. When Kantner went off on a climbing expedition in the Himalayas, Slick cracked: "Paul is climbing Everest because it's the only mountain in the area he can pronounce."

Neil Young was equally harsh about . . . well, Neil Young. "Our parents were into Frank Sinatra, Rosemary Clooney and Perry Como," said Young. "Now, *I'm* Perry Como."

But of all the acid-tongued rock 'n' rollers of the sixties, Grace Slick was the one you really didn't want to cross. She's in her grandmotherly seventies now but she's still got a merciless vision and a wicked tongue in her head. Last year, like millions of others, she took in a Rolling Stones concert.

She wasn't impressed.

"Seeing a Rolling Stones performance," she told a radio interviewer, "is like watching rotting fruit."

Ouch.

I'm sure that somewhere in the underworld, Pierre Berton is laughing like a loon.

HEY, SUZUKI - SORRY ABOUT THAT

Fame is a mask that eats the face.

—JOHN UPDIKE

Shall I tell you why I don't like David Suzuki?

Nah. That's so negative. First, I'll tell you why I do like Edie Falco. Then I'll tell you about my Suzuki aversion.

Edie Falco? You know her—Carmela. Carmela Soprano. She of the spun-candy hairdos, the eagle talon fingernails and the Joisey accent that made me think of a salad fork scrooching down a blackboard. *The Sopranos* is now TV history and so is Carmela. Tony Soprano's wife has metamorphosed and moved on to another TV series called *Nurse Jackie*. Falco's ditched the accent, the nails and the hairdos to play Jackie Peyton—a savvy, tough-as-nails ER nurse in hospital scrubs and a butch haircut, toting a boyfriend for nooners and an eensy-weensy prescription drug habit.

I haven't seen an episode of *Nurse Jackie*, but I'm betting that when I do I won't catch a whiff of mafia mama in Falco's performance. I'm guessing I'll barely recognize her. That's not because of the cosmetic makeover—it's because she's such a fine actor.

Falco doesn't have Angelina Jolie looks or Carol Burnett timing. She can't dance like Catherine Zeta-Jones or purr out a line like Diana Krall, but she's got something more valuable and rare.

Call it stage presence, or charisma, or just the It factor—but when the TV camera pans over to Edie Falco, she owns it. The rest of the cast might as well break for lunch.

And now I'll tell you why I never felt much warmth for David Suzuki.

It's because of something I witnessed at a luggage carousel in the Vancouver Airport about twenty years ago. I was at the tag end of a late night flight from Toronto waiting for my bags to be regurgitated. So were about thirty other passengers, among them David Suzuki.

Well, it happens, right? How many times have you been on an airplane or at a train station when some NHL star or Ottawa politico or TV luminary practically bumps into you? Happens often enough. The correct procedure is just to go about your business—maybe fire off a little smile of recognition, but that's it. We're not in LA or on West Broadway. This is Canada, eh? We don't fuss. And we certainly don't gush.

Except this time, somebody did. An earnest, red-faced, middle-aged, middle-class guy walked up to Suzuki beaming like a lighthouse. He was clearly in awe. He told Suzuki how much he enjoyed *The Nature of Things* and how he'd never missed an edition of the radio show *Quirks and Quarks* and how he thought Suzuki was a Great Canadian and oughtta run for Prime Minister . . .

And Suzuki stoned him. Just stood there, staring woodenly, waiting for the guy to stop talking and go away. After a few seconds of icy silence, the unabashed admirer got the message and slunk off. It was not a nice thing to witness.

And, though it was none of my business, it pissed me off. Sure, the fan was pushing the boundaries, but he meant no harm.

It would have been easy enough for Suzuki to mumble a "Thanks." Wasn't like the guy was hitting on him or looking for a handout.

In any case, it coloured my opinion of one of Canada's most illustrious citizens for, as I say, the past twenty years or so.

Right up until I read an interview with the aforementioned Edie Falco. She was talking to a *Globe and Mail* reporter about her old TV series and what was good about it.

And what was not so good about it. *The Sopranos* was only on the air for six years but it embedded Carmela Soprano's face onto the brainpans of hundreds of millions of people around the world.

"It's hard for me to have so many people know me," Falco said. "I'm a private person. In the morning, I'm walking my dog, I'm taking my kids to school, I've got my hat on. But people are going, 'Oh my god—it's *you!*' and they want some kind of equally excited response. I used to feel obligated to join them. 'OH, THANK YOU!' I'm feeling less obligated now, and I'm afraid it makes me come across as being cold or unkind or ungrateful, which is not the case. It's just a way of holding on to your selfness."

Yeah. I guess I never thought of that.

Bob Dylan is both more famous and blunter about celebrity. "Just because you like my stuff," Dylan said, "doesn't mean I owe you anything."

Good point.

And Suzuki? Sorry about the twenty-year misunderstanding, man.

Not that I'll be coming up to you at the luggage carousel to apologize.

I'LL SUE YOU IN MY DREAMS

So I'm shooting pool with an ex-lawyer I know and in between shots I'm pumping him with various lawyer-type questions because how many chances do you get for free legal advice—even if it is from a guy who's turned in his shingle, so to speak? I am also whining over the latest jurisprudential injustice to bushwhack me. It concerns a book written by an American woman named Cathie Black. The book is a best-seller. She's been on *Oprah* with it. The book is called *Basic Black*.

I, too, have a book called *Basic Black.* It has not propelled me to a spot on Oprah's couch. It is not a best-seller. It is not even a seller. It was published twenty-five years ago and copies of it are as common as papyrus editions of the Dead Sea scrolls. Aside from the dozen or so copies languishing in a cardboard box somewhere at the back of my garage, my *Basic Black* book has pretty much disappeared from the face of the earth.

"Dammit, I own the title *Basic Black,*" I whined to my snooker-shooting Shylock friend. "I used it a quarter-century before this . . . this Cathie come lately! I've got a website called Basic Black! My business card reads 'Basic Black, Inc.' Basic Black is my trademark! I'm going to sue her assets off!"

My ex-lawyer buddy snorted as he potted the pink. "Good luck," he grunted. "Book titles can't be copyrighted. They're not trademarks."

Ah, yes. Trademarks. Strange things, those. And they're not just "marks" either. You know that odd pink hue most house insulation comes in? Don't ever try to put out a line of house insulation that colour. It's trademarked by the Owens-Corning Company.

That classic throaty rumble of a Hell's Angel's "hog"? You'd be a fool to kick-start your cycle if it sounds like that and doesn't have an H-D on the gas tank. The very sound has been copyrighted as a trademark by the Harley-Davidson Motor Company.

It gets crazier in the world of trademarks. A kiddies' daycare in Hallandale, Florida, was threatened with court action by Walt Disney Enterprises a few years back. The daycare facility's crime? Painting five-foot-high caricatures of Mickey, Minnie and Goofy on the walls for the kiddies to enjoy. Disney lawyers didn't enjoy them. Take 'em down or we'll sue, they said. The daycare took them down.

Disney's jealous corporate talons reach beyond American borders. Several years ago, the Ontario town of White River decided to erect a statue of Winnie the Pooh. They didn't know that Disney holds the trademark for the famous bear. The lawyers let White River officials know they faced a massive lawsuit. White River caved.

The irony is that Winnie the Pooh was born in White River—or close to it. The bear that became famous in stories by the British writer A.A. Milne started out as an orphan cub on the White River railway platform during the First World War. He was purchased from a hunter by a Canadian soldier (from Winnipeg, hence the name Winnie) who was shipping out to England. Winnie became a mascot for the Canadian Second Infantry Brigade. When he got too big to handle, the Canadian soldiers donated Winnie to the London Zoo, where A.A. Milne's son saw and fell in love with him. The rest is storybook history.

Long story short, the city fathers of White River thought they had a good and reasonable claim to the image of Winnie the Pooh—until the Disney lawyers came down with both boots and convinced them otherwise.

Thus, all public images, representations and commercial manifestations of a Canadian bear made famous by an English author belong to an American corporation headquartered in California. Ain't free trade wonderful?

Disney isn't the only corporate pit bull when it comes to

anticipated trademark infringement. Recently the city of New York launched a new line of organic cotton shopping bags featuring a logo in the form of a stylized apple.

New York, after all, has been known colloquially as the Big Apple since forever—a natural symbol, right?

Lawyers at Apple, Inc.—the folks who brought you iMacs and iPods and the like—didn't think so. They claim the new NYC logo will "confuse people."

Oh, right. Let me see now . . . is this a city? Or a computer? I'm confused.

It's one thing for lawyers to bluff out daycare workers in Florida, or cross-check municipal officials in small-town Ontario, but New York? The folks there play hardball.

From what I've heard, the Apple, Inc. lawyers have received a two-word response from officials in the Big Apple.

It reads: "Bite me."

PART THREE

CROSS-BORDER SNOOPING

WHAT'S IN A NAME?

Don't you love countries with sensible names? Germany is the land of the Germans, as Scotland is the land of the Scots. England took its name from the Angles; Denmark is home to the Danes as Finland is to Finns.

Some place names serve as personal mementos. Bolivia pays homage to Simon Bolivar. Tasmania commemorates the Dutch explorer Abel Janszoon Tasman. Colombia? A national monument to Christopher Columbus.

Then of course there's our next-door neighbour, also bearing a highly rational, hero-honouring monicker. The United States of . . . America. Named, the history books tell us, after Amerigo Vespucci, a fifteenth-century Italian mariner. The question is: why?

No question that Vespucci existed—only that anybody would ever want to honour him. The man was born in Florence in 1454, died in Seville, Spain, in 1512. In between, he did a little of this and that, including stints at map-making, selling gemstones and hitching rides on ships exploring the New World that had just opened up, bumping along in Columbus's wake and making two voyages along the east coast of South America between 1499 and 1502.

Like Columbus, Vespucci never did actually set his slippered foot on North American soil. Nevertheless he managed somehow to get two continents and what is currently the world's most powerful nation named after him.

Not bad, for a pimp, a blackmailer and a slave-trader—for Vespucci was all of those, too.

Make no mistake—Signor Vespucci was not a nice guy. He bull-shat his way onto a supply ship supporting Columbus's second voyage by pretending to be an expert in celestial navigation. He was lying, but Vespucci usually was. Hustling was what Vespucci did best. Self-promotion was his main product. He boasted to anyone who would listen that he had unlocked the ages-old mystery of longitude—a riddle that had bedeviled mariners for ages. In fact, the problem would not be solved for another three hundred years after his death. That didn't stop Vespucci from adding it to his bogus curriculum vitae. He was never shy about claiming glory—his or anyone else's.

In a famous account of the period known as the Soderini Letter (author unknown, but sounding suspiciously like you-know-who), the writer describes the New World as populated by giants, cannibals and sexually insatiable Amazons. The letter also describes the exploits of one Amerigo Vespucci at great length and in glowing terms, and it attributes the discovery of the New World and its wonders not to Christopher Columbus, but to (surprise, surprise)—our friend Amerigo.

Bogus or not, the letter convinced a German by the name of Martin Waldseemuller, the premier cartographer of the era. He quite literally put Vespucci on the map. He took his name and Latinized it to *Americus Vespucius.* And then, because other continents—Asia, Africa, Australia—had feminine names, he feminized Americus.

And that's how we got America—North, South and United States of.

But half a millennium on, the story still carries a suspicious whiff of dubiety. Whoever heard of a continent or a country adopting the first, rather than the last name of its hero? It's Bolivia, not Simonia. Tasmania, not Abelland. Colombia, not Cristoforia.

So how come George W. Bush wasn't forty-third president of the United States of Vespuccia?

Some observers contend we're barking up the wrong historical tree altogether. They claim we've got the wrong Amerigo. Sylvain Fribourg, an amateur historian living in California, points out that more than three decades before Columbus's famous first voyage, a well-heeled Welshman and member of the British Royal Court was financing fishing expeditions to this part of the planet. He was the chief sponsor of John Cabot's historic voyage to Newfoundland in 1497. His name appeared on maps that Columbus (and undoubtedly Vespucci) saw years before the *Nina*, the *Pinta* and the *Santa Maria* set sail from Cadiz. That name? Richard . . . Amerike.

It's a fine old Welsh name. There's even an Amerike(can) coat of arms. It's made up of stars. And stripes.

It would be nice if someone could definitively prove our neighbours intended to honour the long-forgotten British merchant. Amerike the savvy Welshman is a more savoury character to hang a country's name on than Amerigo the two-bit Florentine hustler.

Besides, with political correctness and all, how long could it be before we'd have to sit through baseball games starting off with thousands of fans intoning the words to "Vespuccia the Beautiful"?

‹FILL IN THE BLANK›
ENUF FER YA?

Everybody talks about the weather, but nobody does anything about it.

—MARK TWAIN

Good one, Mark—and all the funnier for being true. We do talk about the weather. Indeed, with sex, politics and religion pretty much off the table for polite discourse, the weather is one of the few conversational constants we can fall back on.

Not that our weather observations tend to be inspirational. Usually they run along the lines of "Phew/Brr . . . hot/cold/dry/wet enough fer ya?"

Or, "Man, that was some rain/snow/wind we had last night, eh?"

I know of only one weather conversation that didn't go well. It occurred between then-prime minister Pierre Trudeau and his finance minister, Jean Chrétien. Slipping in beside his boss on a campaign bus, Chrétien observed that it "Sure was raining outside."

Trudeau replied icily that he was "encouraged" to learn that it was raining "outside," as it would be rather inconvenient if it were raining "inside."

Monsieur Crankypants Trudeau aside, most Canadians are far too polite (and meteorologically long-suffering) to cold-shoulder anybody's weather observations, no matter how banal. Fact is, we tend to revel in such stuff. And nothing gives us greater pleasure than that annual autumnal ritual in which we attempt to divine What Kind of a Winter We're in For.

Canadians have two meteorological camps to which we can pledge allegiance: Environment Canada and *The Old Farmer's Almanac.*

Environment Canada is reserved for those among us who see ourselves as rational and scientifically minded. The government agency employs millions of dollars worth of satellites, radar and other technological gewgaws to keep us abreast of the latest news in isotherms, highs, lows, fronts, troughs and other meteorological phenomena.

And then there's *The Old Farmer's Almanac,* a hoary compendium of gardening nostrums, astrological trivia and sundry ephemera that's been published every year since 1792. But that's just window dressing. What *The Old Farmer's Almanac* is really about is weather prognostication. The *Almanac* soothsayers lay out exactly what we can expect to encounter when we open our front doors.

Almanac forecasters don't rely on sophisticated technology. They lean toward sunspots, tide tables and the position of the planets to deduce the coming weather patterns. "In essence," the editor writes, "these pages are unchanged since 1792 . . . the long columns of numbers and symbols reveal all of nature's precision, rhythm and glory."

Yeah, swell—but how accurate is *The Old Farmer's Almanac?*

Pretty darn accurate, according to, er, *The Old Farmer's Almanac.* Editor Peter Geiger claims the guide is on the money 80 to 85 percent of the time.

This is a much better batting average than David Phillips would ever claim on behalf of the outfit he works for. David Phillips? Chief climatologist with Environment Canada. Phillips says that even with its supercomputers and a wealth of data, Environment Canada is leery of predicting anything more than ten days ahead. Whereas *The Old Farmer's Almanac* ball gazers blithely roll the dice for up to two years in advance.

Which brings us to the coming winter. According to *The Old Farmer's Almanac,* we're in for a bad one.

Really bad.

It says that this winter, most of Canada will experience minus 40-degree weather or worse. It even uses the word "catastrophic."

Scared? David Phillips and the folks at Environment Canada

aren't. "We never really advise people to bet the family farm on [our forecasts] because it is a bit of a crapshoot." I guess we'll find out soon enough who's right about this particular winter.

Speaking of crapshoots, I should point out that *The Old Farmer's Almanac* comes with a hole punched through the top of it right next to the spine. In earlier years, this hole facilitated hanging the *Almanac* from a nail in the outhouse wall.

Pioneer recycling. When a reader was finished reading a page of the *Almanac*, the person could rip it off and, er, dispose of it appropriately.

Reminds me of the letter US president Harry Truman fired off to a theatre reviewer who panned an acting performance by Truman's daughter.

"I am sitting in the smallest room in the house with your review before me," wrote Truman. "Shortly, it will be behind me."

Let's hope that, come spring, we can all do the same thing with the *Farmer's Almanac* winter weather forecast.

COMMENT DIT-ON "BEAUTY, EH"?

So I'm trapped behind the chip dip at this soiree in Kitsilano. Planted firmly before me in high heels and a low top is this woman I barely know who is reciting her resumé, not that anybody asked. She lets it drop that she speaks four languages, including French, then she adds with a sniff: "Parisian French . . . not Québécois. They speak horrible French in Quebec."

And I know it's uncharitable and certainly un-Christian, but my first instinct is to reach for a bowl of *crème glacée* and dump it all over her pretentious *tête*.

I don't, of course—I'm a Canadian (as is she). But the atmosphere cools and I start planning my getaway, though I'm not sure why I'm suddenly feeling protective and defensive about Canada's French. God knows they don't want or need my (assume defensive position: French word incoming)—patronage.

Besides, our Canadian French confreres have been under assault from another, more unlikely source of late: France.

At a convention of historians and politicos in Quebec City it was revealed that, contrary to what we learned at school and what every séparatiste believes in his heart, Quebec was not a tragic concession cruelly torn from the breast of France and awarded to Britain back in 1763. According to modern historians Quebec was more of an unprofitable pain in the derriere that the French couldn't wait to unload.

"We heard that we weren't conquered," says Quebec senator Serge Joyal. "The British just waited for the French to give us away. That's shocking to many people. The French didn't want us."

Such a revelation goes a long way toward explaining the sniggering and supercilious attitude the European French have long reserved for Quebec. The French, who centuries ago raised snobbery to an art form, have always been especially disdainful of the Québécois. They regarded them as bumptious colonial rubes who dressed badly and talked funny.

Especially talked funny. "Joual" is the name of the Montreal dialect most commonly associated with French Canadians—the word is a corruption of the word for horse, "cheval." In the old days, the French hid behind their fans every time a Québécois moved his or her lips—*très drôle*. Now it seems the French may have to learn to laugh out of the other side of their mouths.

It's because of a movie that's taken France by storm. It's called *Bienvenue chez les Ch'tis*—which translates as Welcome to Ch'tisland. The movie is about a typical southern French urban snob, a postal worker, who gets sent—exiled—to the far north of France where the inhabitants are, well, hicks. They come off as stupid, backward, malingering drunkards. Ch'tis is the dialect they speak, and it's incomprehensible to outsiders—even other Frenchmen. The snob's opening line to the first Ch'tis speaker he meets: "Is there something wrong with your jaw?"

It's a feel-good movie that exploits a hackneyed theme: cultivated sophisticate from the Big City gradually learns something about the real values of life from an encounter with unvarnished sons of the soil. He and the audience come to adore and respect these lovable, honest, surprisingly canny country folk.

Kind of a Gallic version of *Corner Gas*.

As a premise for a French movie *Bienvenue chez les Ch'tis* should have gone over like a bowl of poutine at the Ritz. In fact, it's a smash. More than twenty million French citizens have lined up to see the film. And they're attending not to make mock of the rustic characters on the screen, they're coming to admire them—and the funny way they talk.

Some French observers are mystified—and more than a little worried. Michel Wieviorka, a Paris sociologist, frets that the film "celebrates a France that is inward-looking, fearful of the future and lazy." He also describes the characters as "franchouillard," which is to say, "redneck."

Heck, we Anglos can help him with that. No need to fret—the French have simply discovered their inner Don Cherry. If they work at it real hard, they might someday be ready for Bob and Doug McKenzie.

Wonder what the French is for "Beauty, eh?"

CANADA:
TALL POPPIES PROHIBITED

American applauds with glee the highest climber of the
tree.
Englishman has half a mind the tree is not the proper
kind.
Canadian with tiny frown takes an axe and chops it
down.

A poet by the name of Robin Skelton wrote those lines. Mister Skelton was a Cambridge graduate who flew with the Royal Air Force in India. He was also an authority on Irish literature, a poet, a world-class translator of ancient Greek and Roman and a practising witch. In most countries, Robin Skelton would have been a household name. Alas, he chose Canada for a homeland and died largely unknown.

We don't do heroes well in this country—unless they carry a hockey stick. As someone once said, "Americans remember where they were when Kennedy was shot; Canadians remember where they were when Henderson scored."

You don't need hockey smarts to be a hero in America. Take the case of Chesley Sullenberger. Just a few years back, Mister Sullenberger—Sully to his friends—was a quiet, retiring commercial pilot for US Airways. But then on January 15, 2009, the engines on the plane he was flying from New York to Charlotte, North Carolina, sucked in a couple of Canada geese and seized up. Against advice from the experts, Sully landed the plane in the Hudson River. All 153 people on board survived.

And Chesley Sullenberger's life changed overnight. He was a Certified American Hero. He got a tickertape parade in his hometown of Danville, California. He was a guest on *Larry King*. The program *60 Minutes* did a profile on him.

All because he fulfilled part of his job description: he landed his plane safely. How, one wonders, would that have been handled if it had happened in Canada?

We don't have to wonder. We have Air Canada flight 143.

On July 23, 1983, AC 143 was en route from Montreal to Edmonton with sixty-one passengers and eight crew aboard. About halfway through the flight—over Red Lake, Ontario, at 41,000 feet—the cockpit crew heard something no cockpit crew wants to hear: a warning buzzer indicating a fuel pressure problem. Seconds later, another buzzer indicating another fuel pressure problem followed by complete failure of one engine.

No problem. They could easily divert to Winnipeg and execute a single-engine landing. All pilots are trained for that.

Then came another warning buzzer followed by a sound no one in the cockpit had heard before. It was a loud, ominous *bonnnnnnng*.

It was the "All Engines Out" alarm. The instrument panel dimmed and went blank. The Boeing 737, all two hundred feet of it, was flying—*gliding*—over northern Ontario wilderness. A hundred-plus tonnes of steel, people and Samsonite luggage does not a good glider make. Even though it was eight miles up, the plane was settling fast. They'd already dropped 5,000 feet while covering just ten nautical miles. It didn't take the cockpit crew long to figure out that the plane would never make it to Winnipeg.

But flight 143 had two aces in the hole: the pilot, Captain Robert Pearson, was a former glider pilot. And the first officer Maurice Quintal knew the area. He used to fly out of Gimli, Manitoba, which was a lot closer than Winnipeg. Quintal radioed Winnipeg suggesting the air force base at Gimli as an alternative.

Which would have been a no-brainer if there still was an air force base at Gimli, but the base had been decommissioned and turned into a local drag strip. What's more, today was "Family Day," meaning car races on the former runway surrounded by

Winnebagos, station wagons, picnic blankets, barbecues and lots of civilians.

Not exactly a perfect landing site, but the only one they had.

Miraculously, using all his glider-training skills, Captain Pearson wrestled the stricken, lumbering airliner down the strip. He blew out two tires, scraped up the plane's nose and gave several hundred picnickers the thrill of a lifetime, but not one spectator and, aside for a few bumps and bruises, not a single passenger or crew member was hurt.

The Canadian twist? Flight 143 had run out of fuel in mid-air. Why? Because Canada was in the process of converting to the metric system at the time. Someone had screwed up. Instead of 22,000 *kilograms*, they took off with 22,000 *pounds* of fuel. Enough to get them almost halfway to their destination.

Actually there was another Canadian twist to the story. Remember the hero treatment America gave Chesley Sullenberger for landing his plane in the Hudson? Air Canada rewarded Captain Pearson with . . . a six-month suspension. First Officer Quintal was suspended for two weeks.

Well, it's their own fault for working for Air Canada. Now if they'd played for the Edmonton Oilers . . .

AMERICA:
ARMED AND DANGEROUS

Most bizarre headline I've seen this week? *Los Angeles Times*: "Two Shot in Bicycle Drive-by Outside South L.A. House."

Bicycle drive-by? American hit men are now pedalling *bicycles* to and from their assignations? What next—pogo sticks? Skateboards?

Don't bet against it. When you put Americans and their sacrosanct Right to Bear Arms into the same equation the outcome is anybody's guess. Take the man California cops found slumped over and bleeding heavily from what was euphemistically described as "massive groin damage" caused by a gunshot. The guy also tried to blame "drive-by shooters" for his predicament, but the cops noticed a sawed-off shotgun lying nearby and figured out the truth. The "victim"—a member of an LA gang—had been practising his macho moves by jamming the shotgun in his waistband and sneering into a mirror. Somehow he managed to discharge both barrels into his, ahem, pants.

The good news is, he didn't die. The headline should have read: "Man Blows Brains Out, Lives."

Then there was the story out of Harrold, Texas, where the school district officials have voted in favour of arming their elementary school teachers with concealed handguns.

There are 110 kids enrolled in the Harrold Independent School, ranging from kindergarten to grade twelve. They already live with constant camera surveillance and a school-wide alarm system. Each student must swipe a card to enter and exit the school. Teachers have access to a kill button that instantly locks all school doors.

Not enough, the school board deemed. "I can lead my children from a tornado," intones school superintendent David Thweatt, "I can lead them from a fire. I can lead them from a toxic spill quickly. I cannot lead them from an active shooter."

Right. And the grade nine music teacher swapping bullets with a gun-toting maniac over the students' heads? That should work out well.

To be fair, not every adult in Harrold, Texas, is a mouth-breathing idiot. Gayle Fallon, president of the Houston Federation of Teachers, called the new policy "embarrassing" and "the stupidest move that I have seen done in public education." She warns that all those guns in a school setting constitute a tragedy waiting to happen. "Children have one thing in common," says Ms. Fallon. "They are all fascinated by guns, and they will play with them if they find them."

And not just children. About 30,000 Americans use a gun to kill themselves or others each year. Another 75,000 or so merely cripple themselves like Joe Macho, above. By comparison, about 1,200 Canadians die from gunshot wounds each year—still appalling, but a statistic that the city of Detroit, say, would, er, kill for.

It's not because Canadians are smarter, it's because it's a whole lot harder to pack heat in Victoria, BC, than it is in Buena Vista, Virginia. You can't buy a Saturday night special in a Canadian pawnshop. And we don't have a National Rifle Association to bloviate about Canadians' natural-born right to carry AK-47 assault rifles with armour-piercing shells into the supermarket.

Canada—indeed the rest of the world—is not nearly so insane about arming its civilians as our pistol-packin' friends to the south—but that doesn't mean we're immune. A few days after the grisly murder and decapitation of a passenger on a Greyhound bus in Manitoba, some gun nut wrote a letter to the editor of my local paper opining that the whole incident could have been avoided "if just one passenger on that bus had been carrying a gun."

Uh-huh. And if that one passenger happened to be the killer—

sporting, say a MAC-10 machine pistol (a thousand rounds per minute) instead of a machete . . .

An old teacher of mine once cautioned me that there are three topics you should never raise at the dinner table: sex, politics and religion. If you happen to be breaking bread with a Right Thinking American, I'd add "guns" to that list. Tempers will flare and no minds will be changed.

My second-favourite news story of late? The one about bridegroom Jeff Nichols of San Diego lifting the hem of his wife's wedding gown to retrieve her garter so he could toss it into the crowd, only to encounter a thigh holster, complete with loaded revolver.

Jeff's blushing bride is a police officer, you see. His response: "Oops, wrong leg." Much merriment all around.

My question: Who the hell wants to live in a country where it's considered amusing when the blushing bride wears a loaded pistol under her wedding gown?

DON'T JUDGE A ROOK
BY ITS LOVER

When I Google "homeless people" in my brain, my memory
bank serves up two indelible hits. One of them is an incident
that happened to me in 1983 in downtown New York. Coming out
of the Iroquois Hotel I asked the doorman for the nearest subway
stop. He raised an elegant, white-gloved hand to point me in the right
direction.

I remember that immaculate white glove, index finger extended,
because right behind it, just ever-so-slightly out of focus, was a
street hobo hunched over a heat grate. He was living in a cardboard
refrigerator carton.

A generation ago, and homeless people were already unremark-
able—at least in New York.

My second "homeless moment" happened in downtown
Vancouver while I was stopped at a crosswalk waiting for pedestrians to cross. I must have been engrossed in some dreary mental
daydreaming because one of the pedestrians—a street person by
his grubby garb—stopped right in front of my car and stared at me.
When he got my attention he put the thumb and index finger of his
right hand to the corners of his lips and pushed his face into a grin.

"Smile," he was telling me.

Somebody without a home and probably no idea where he would

eat that night—somebody I'd been too self-obsessed to even notice—was urging me to "Cheer up."

Yet another timely reminder of how easy it is to "disappear" the homeless—and also how dangerous it is to judge anybody just by the way they look.

Suppose, for instance, I could whisk you to Dupont Circle, a rather grungy urban park in downtown Washington, DC. Chances are that sooner rather than later we'd run into Tom Murphy. Tom's a regular in the park and not, frankly, much to look at. He's forty-nine but appears older. He usually wears a grubby sweater, a pair of Nike sweatpants that are out at the knee and running shoes well past their best-before date. Oh, Tom is also black, unshaven and hirsutely disorganized under his ratty St. Louis Cardinals baseball cap.

Chances are even better that when we meet him, Tom will be more than somewhat thick of tongue and/or bloodshot of eye because, to quote from the Mr. Bojangles song, he "drinks a bit." It would be childishly easy to dismiss Tom Murphy as just another urban alky bum waiting for his welfare cheque.

And it would be wrong.

You may have noticed that Tom likes to sit by one of the many stone chessboards that adorn Dupont Circle. Perhaps you think it would be generous and liberal of you to offer to play a few easy moves with him.

Don't get comfortable. Tom Murphy will whip your butt before you've warmed the chair.

Tom Murphy will not only beat you at chess, he will do it in ten minutes or less. He is not just a chess genius, he is a wizard at a hyperfast form of the game called "Blitz." In Blitz, each player has a maximum of five minutes to make all his moves. At the end of ten minutes a buzzer goes and the game is over.

David Mehler, who runs Washington's Chess Center, has been watching Tom Murphy for years. "He has a very fast mind," Mehler told a *Washington Post* reporter, "and he sees combinations quickly. He calculates very quickly."

Just how good is Tom Murphy? Good enough to rate the title of "expert," which is the second highest ranking in North America. In 2005 he entered a Blitz championship and came in fifteenth.

In the world.

If he bought himself a suit and tie, a shave and a haircut, Tom Murphy could probably earn a decent living as a chess professional—certainly as an instructor. But he prefers life in Dupont Circle among the pigeons and the other indigents. There, he plays for booze money, charging anywhere from two to five dollars a game against all comers.

Maybe Tom Murphy's presence in the park serves another purpose too. Maybe, like the homeless guy in front of my car, teaching me to Get Over Myself—maybe he serves to remind us not to judge a book by its cover. Or a rook by its lover.

After all, if a scruffy vagrant with holes in his socks can clean your clock at one of the most difficult games in the world, what else don't you know about him?

OLYMPIC FUN 'N' GAMES

*Serious sport has nothing to do with fair play. It is
bound up with hatred, jealousy, boastfulness, disregard
of all rules and sadistic pleasure in witnessing violence:
in other words, it is war minus the shooting.*

—GEORGE ORWELL

Obviously George never spent much time in the Great White
North. In Canada, we don't do sports like that. Canadians play
nice. Look how nice we've played with the IOC after they graciously
deigned to let us host the 2010 Winter Olympics.

When they asked us to build brand new multi-million-dollar
sports venues, we reached for our cheque book. When they complained that the Sea to Sky Highway through the mountains was too
twisty we built them a new one.

As for Olympic-themed clothing, we kind of hoped they'd give
the nod to our local, traditional, Cowichan sweaters that we've
bestowed upon everyone from the Queen to Vladimir Putin—but
the IOC fixers nixed that. Said they could get coats cheaper from an
"approved" supplier back east. We said, "Hey, no problem!" as we
did when they outsourced those official Olympics mittens. They were
huge best-sellers. Which is great news for the Chinese manufacturers
who shipped them to us by the boatload.

When the IOC decreed that all Olympic torchbearers would
wear an outfit that made them look like fugitive bakers or maybe

extras from a *Casper the Friendly Ghost* movie, Canadians didn't utter a peep of protest.

And when they announced that the torchbearers would be forbidden to wear any other advertising whatsoever—that even the Nike swooshes on their running shoes had to be duct-taped over—we just smiled and bent over a little further. Hey, why not? The IOC said they'd even pay for the duct tape!

Admittedly, the Vancouver Symphony Orchestra got a little uppity when the Olympic Organizing Committee told them the VSO would be essentially "lip-synching" their performance at the opening ceremonies. The conductor had a hissy fit and cried foul. "I regarded that as fraudulent and withdrew," the conductor said. What a grandstander! Didn't he know there's historical precedent for faking the music at the opening of the Olympics? In Beijing the officials yanked seven-year-old singer Yang Peiyi who was slated to sing *Ode to the Motherland*. At the last minute they replaced her with nine-year-old Lin Miaoke. Oh, the seven-year-old could sing like a bird, but . . . well, she had these crooked teeth, see? So the officials taped her voice and got the more photogenic Lin Miaoke to lip-synch for the ceremony. Wouldn't you know it—some nosey Western reporter figured it out and spilled the beans.

Can't blame the Chinese really—they're pretty green when it comes to international sports protocol. Canadians have a history of playing nice with the big boys.

Once upon a time we had money-making National Hockey League franchises in Winnipeg and Quebec City, but NHL commissioner Gary Bettman, a New Yorker, didn't care for that. He yanked the teams, relocating them in the US. You can see his reasoning. Much more sensible to situate pro franchises in hockey hotbeds like Arizona and Florida.

The important thing—and I think this is probably what the IOC likes best about Canada as a venue—is our respectfulness. And boy, are we respectful. We're so respectful we won't even let foreigners into the country who look like they might not be respectful enough. Last December, Canadian border guards at Vancouver grabbed up Amy Goodman and questioned her for over an hour. So who's Amy Goodman? Taliban operative? Al-Qaeda suicide bomber?

Worse. She's host of a show called *Democracy Now* on National

Public Radio in the US. The border guys were nervous about the fact that this 120-pound middle-aged woman broadcaster was planning *to give a speech* in Vancouver. After an hour-long grilling, the gist of which was one question: *was she planning to say anything negative about the Olympics?* they grudgingly let her into the country. But only on a forty-eight-hour pass, mind. Can't be too careful with these 120-pound, middle-aged female radio people.

You know the old saying: you can't make an omelette without breaking a few eggs—and the 2010 Winter Olympics is some omelette. The price tag, we're assured as of this writing, is $6 billion, but I'm taking side bets that the final bill, when all security and infrastructure costs are toted up, will be well north of $10 billion—you read it here first.

But look on the bright side: there is life—and black ink—after these international bashes. Look at Montreal. As of this writing that city is officially free of its Expo 67-generated debt.

And it only took forty-two years.

TOO HOT FOR THIS FROSTBACK

*A**rrgghh*! Another wretched Canadian winter sinking its icy talons into my chilblained carcass. More treacherous weeks of power blackouts, balky batteries, snow-bloated driveways and black-iced roads. I'm getting too old for this. Isn't there some alternative?

Well . . . there's Arizona. Fate, being the fickle-fingered fortune teller she is, sent me a letter from a Winnipeg law firm last September. How would I like to speak at their winter retreat to be held in November at—I blink and rub my eyes to make sure I'm not hallucinating—the Westin Kierland Resort and Spa in Scottsdale, Arizona?

Scottsdale. Part of the sprawling urban agglomeration known (inaccurately but universally) as Phoenix. Where the November daytime temperature routinely soars in the high and sunny twenties. Phoenix. Where Google tells me they've had a grand total of less than three inches of rain *so far this year*. Phoenix, where to explain the concept of falling snow to the natives you'd have to resort to CBC video footage and maybe sock puppets wearing ear muffs. A few days in Phoenix, Arizona, for a winter-blitzed Canadian struggling through the nether end of November. How sweet is that?

Kind of bittersweet, as it turns out. The airport gauntlet would bring any traveller down. It is the usual horror show of security rent-a-thugs ordering crippled geriatrics to take off their shoes while their cohorts gleefully pounce on such terrorist paraphernalia as eyebrow tweezers, crochet hooks and half-spent tubes of Colgate toothpaste.

I watch a security goon suspiciously rub his grubby thumb over the war medals on the lapel of the jacket of a war veteran being "processed." What's he think they are—al-Qaeda grenades? He grunts and moves on to wand/grope the next patsy in the lineup. Not our finest hour, airport security.

Scottsdale, when we finally arrive, is kind of odd. As Gertrude Stein once said of Oakland, California, "There's no 'there' there." The airport limo whisks us along wide boulevards that all look the same—here a palm tree, there some sage brush, and once in a while a cartoon-like saguaro cactus, looming up like a prickly pitchfork—all of it intersected by long chutes of concrete walls behind which squat, one-storey homes peek out. Scottsdale doesn't have enough water to grow grass, so it substitutes a kind of pink gravel that gives the city the effect of a huge rambling terrarium. I half expect to see a giant tortoise rumble out on to the boulevard.

The valley that Phoenix nestles in is home to nearly four million Americans, many of them refugees from snow-blasted states to the north and east. There's also a fair representation of ex-Californians in the valley because houses are way cheaper in Phoenix than they are in Governor Schwarzenegger's fiefdom. Think the Grand Canyon State is all good ol' boys and Navaho reservations? Surprise. Arizona is almost 25 percent Hispanic.

One of the treasures of the Phoenix area is tucked into the hills and hard to find. It is Taliesin West, a house built by the famous architect Frank Lloyd Wright. It's a treasure because it is unlike anything else you're likely to see in the area—or anywhere else, come to that. Whimsical and surprising, at turns rambling and cozy, it fits into the landscape as snug as a cowboy boot in a stirrup.

More important, Taliesin pays homage to the native tribes that lived here for thousands of years before the white man came. The desert around Taliesin West has not been razed, paved and compartmentalized into tract houses—yet. It is here that you can feel the true charm of the land—the cacti, the desert birds, the stark, snaggle-toothed mountains that rim the perimeter. And the spectacular sunsets.

Yep, that's why we're all here—native Phoenicians and frost-weary Winnipeg lawyers alike—to get a taste of that lovely November sun. And winter's the time to sample Phoenix sunshine. Don't try this trick in summer. You really can fry an egg on a Phoenix sidewalk in August. TV film crews do it routinely on slow (hot) news days.

How hot does it get? They hit 53 Celsius a couple of times last August. That's 125 Fahrenheit for the unconverted—hotter than hell on anybody's thermometer. And they weren't just a couple of rogue spikes. My taxi driver told me that last summer Phoenix had thirty-five days where the temperature hit 110 or over.

Was it always this hot in Phoenix? No. Before it became the second-fastest-growing city in the country, Phoenix was merely infernally hot. Now, it's insane.

Thanks to the endless new acres of concrete, rooftops and a maze of buildings that blocks wind, the summer heat gets trapped, reflected and absorbed. Add to that the mandatory air conditioners (that kick heated air back into the atmosphere while they deplete the energy grid) and you've got an escalating nightmare. Move to Phoenix? No thanks. I'd rather live in Aklavik.

Nice place to visit, but I wouldn't want to fry there.

WACKY ROADSIDE ATTRACTIONS

Did you see the news story about Serbia on CNN? It was a feature report about how Serbians have taken to erecting huge, reverential statues of cultural heroes along roadsides, in parks and on public squares.

Which isn't all that weird on the face of it. Most societies erect public statuary commemorating notable historical figures. What's a little different about Serbia's approach is the subject matter. The village of Banatski Sokolac, for instance, has statues of Tarzan. And Rocky Balboa. And the character portrayed by martial-arts film star Bruce Lee. These people aren't Serbian. They aren't even real people. What's the deal?

"My generation can't find role models at home," one Serbian artist explained.

The article got my attention not so much because of the goofy statues, but because CNN thought it was newsworthy. You want wacky roadside attractions, CNN? Don't waste your money sending a film crew to Serbia. Point 'em north. When it comes to wacky roadside attractions Canada is Tarzan and Rocky and Bruce Lee combined.

Let's take a coast-to-coast tour, cherrypicking just a few Canadian roadside attractions. There's . . . well, cherries, for starters. The town of Lancer, Saskatchewan, has a twenty-foot steel chokecherry sculpture on the main street. Animals? How about Huskie the Muskie—a giant leaping muskellunge on the outskirts of Kenora, Ontario. There's also the Wawa goose, Creston's Bigfoot and who could overlook Ralph, the giant green grasshopper that looms over Ogema, SK?

Well, maybe the folks of Edson, Alberta, could. Those poor wretches are forced to dwell in the shadow of a gargantuan concrete squirrel that stands poised over their town, ready to crack it like a walnut. Squirrel's name is Eddie. (Eddie. Edson. Geddit?)

Lots of towns—Boissevain, MB, Kitimat, BC, Plaster Rock, NB, and Niagara Falls, ON, to name but four—have erected outsized bear statues, but not too many towns have a beluga whale monument (Tadoussac, QC, makes the cut). Jasper has a Bighorn Sheep and Victoria has a Big Pink Fish. Citizens of South Dildo, NF, can point with pride to the huge whale head breaching out of the gravel on the shoulder of the main road into town.

A giant whale? South Dildo? You'd think . . . never mind.

Sometimes the statuary erected by Canadians invites the question "what the hell were they thinking?" The town of Vonda, SK, for example, has replicated a two-storey whisky still by the town's approach. Who paid for that—the Vonda Bootleggers Cartel?

Some Canadian monuments look like they might have been inspired by chaps who spent rather too much time sampling the output of the Vonda still. Edmonton has a statue of a blue buffalo wearing a kilt. The town of South River, ON, displays a sculpture that looks like a mess of lobster claws welded onto two spears of asparagus. That one baffles even the South River elders. The plaque identifies the sculpture as "The ??"

I don't know if it's the fecundity of the Canadian imagination or just the long winters but Canadian Roadside Attractions range from the profound (Brotherhood of Mankind, Calgary) to the prosaic (Eugene the Prospector, Bodo, AB); from the ethereal (Flying Saucer, Moonbeam, ON) to the mundane (Bracebridge's giant pencil).

Some towns exhibit memorials that could only be Canadian. Beardmore, ON, boasts a statue of the World's Largest Snowman, while the town of Duncan, BC, spent its advertising budget on a giant hockey stick, 205 feet long and 31 tons in weight.

My all-time favourite Canadian roadside monument? I lean toward the structure that graces the outskirts of the town of Macklin, which is about a hundred klicks south of Lloydminster, SK. It stands thirty feet high, pure white and looks . . . vaguely sexy . . . something like an hourglass, although if you tilt your head and squint your eyes you might think you're looking at a lithe and limbless nude torso.

Don't get excited. It depicts a bunnock—which is to say, it's a statue dedicated to a horse's anklebone. Bunnock is a big deal in Macklin. It's not only a bone, it's the name of a game that has European roots going back four hundred years. Early Russian and German settlers brought the game to Saskatchewan back in the 1800s. Bunnock is kind of a cross between bowling and curling, except less exciting. Basically, a team lines up to throw horse anklebones at the other team's horse anklebones. The winning team is the one that knocks over the most horse knucklebones.

Remember what I said about long winters?

Sounds dopey, but each August, visiting teams from as far away as Japan and Australia travel to Macklin to compete for prizes in the World Bunnock Championships. It pumps an estimated half a million dollars into the Macklin economy.

Just another wacky roadside attraction? If anybody's having a horse laugh, it's the folks in Macklin.

MAULED BY MALLS

In Xanadu did Kubla Khan
A stately pleasure dome decree.
—SAMUEL TAYLOR COLERIDGE

In the spring of 1938 a short, pudgy Austrian immigrant name of Victor Gruen waddled hopefully down the gangplank of a ship newly docked in New York harbour. His timing was not propitious— America was coming off the Great Depression and heading toward a World War. The guy had eight dollars US in one pocket and an architect's degree in another. Nevertheless that Austrian immigrant probably did more to change the physical world you live in than any other human being of our time.

Gruen was a socialist as well as an architect, and he greatly missed the warmth and conviviality of the typical European towns he grew up in—the cheery cafés, the bustling plazas, the common, cozy meeting grounds. He resolved to bring some of that magic to cold, car-ridden North America, so Victor Gruen invented the modern indoor shopping mall.

Boy, did he screw that up.

Today, just about every medium-sized town and all of the big ones have at least one indoor shopping mall—several acres of parking stalls surrounding a blank-walled complex consisting of inward-facing storefronts, air-conditioned in the summer, heated in the winter.

And all dedicated to separating people from their money.

Like dinosaurs, the shopping malls dominated the terrain they overlooked by virtue of their sheer size. Traditional downtown retail districts shrivelled and shrank before the mighty malls with their fountains and food courts and near-endless siren enticements for consumers. But somewhere around the turn of the twenty-first century the shopping malls assumed another characteristic of the dinosaur. They began to go extinct.

Not surprising really. The enclosed shopping mall was a rarified and artificial creation from the get-go. It was dedicated to the proposition that consumers would always be ready to nibble and that each year they would always happily spend more than they did last year.

Unlimited growth forever: the modus operandi of the cancer cell.

Your typical shopping mall has another fatal genetic flaw: almost everything it sells is unessential. Name-brand jeans? Designer sunglasses? Pastel-hued cellphones? Two-hundred-dollar running shoes?

As social scientist Henry Fairlie puts it: "The most important fact about our shopping malls is that we do not need most of what they sell."

Which may work when times are flush, but it's not so hot when the economy is hurting.

Our next-door neighbours are feeling the pinch more than Canadians. Over four hundred of the two thousand largest US malls have closed in the past two years. The plight of US malls has become so grim it's inspired a website. Deadmalls.com was created by a couple of guys who decided it was archeologically important to document the abandoned malls for future students of American civilization before those malls disappeared entirely.

Dinosaurs were doomed at least partly because they were cursed with fatally small brains; the powers behind malls have a stronger survival instinct. For the past ten years or so, mall promoters have been reinventing their product, encouraging visitors to use the premises for walking and jogging, book signings and karaoke get-togethers. Some offer their facilities for laser tag, paintball for teenagers and merry-go-rounds for the kiddies. "Parents still need to entertain their kids," an industry analyst says. "Teenagers still need a place to hang out. Adults need a place to walk, out of the elements. Workers still need to buy their coffee."

All true—but a bit of a scale-back from the high times when supermalls confidently promised "the ultimate in 'shoppertainment.'"

I didn't make up that grotesque line; it's a quote from Larry Siegel, the man in charge of the nascent Xanadu mall currently a-building in East Rutherford, New Jersey. Xanadu is scheduled to be truly a monster mall—2.4 million square feet—with an indoor ski slope, a for-real fishing pond, the largest Ferris wheel in North America—even a thirty-foot-high chocolate waterfall.

Xanadu broke ground in 2004 and was slated to open to the public in August 2009, but what with the recession and all the grand opening had to be pushed back to late November. Then it was delayed again. Right now, Xanadu is now scheduled to open "sometime next year."

Or not.

TROPICAL CANADA? WHY NOT?

Here's a want ad you don't often come across:

> For Sale: One tropical island in the Bahamas, 184 kilometres long by 2 kilometres wide, situated 80 kilometres east of Nassau. Terms: Ninety-nine-year lease. Price: One dollar.

This is not a late April Fool's joke. The island of Eleuthera was actually available to a select Canadian buyer for the above-mentioned terms back in 1985. The prospective purchaser? Quebec. The province's then-minister of tourism under René Lévesque had painstakingly hammered out a tentative deal with the prime minister of the Bahamas. Quebec would assume ownership of Eleuthera for the princely outlay of one loonie—and a promise to "hire local labour" where possible. Catches, tricks or loopholes? None.

Naturellement, the Quebec cabinet turned the deal down.

Well, that's Quebec for ya, is it not? Perverse. Masochistic. Ever on the lookout for a new and different way to shaft itself with the short end of the hockey stick. Man, you give the rest of Canada an opportunity to bag a brand new, tropical paradise and we'd be all over it like suntan oil on a bald guy's head, right?

Wrong. Ottawa had its chance to adopt a tropical paradise. Not just one island either—two whole chains of them. Back in 1987, a delegation of politicians from the Turks and Caicos Islands in the

Caribbean actually visited Ottawa, hats in hand, openly seeking a shotgun marriage.

They wanted us to take them in, people! They begged to become part of Canada. They would bring to us thirty surf-massaged islands festooned with bedazzling sand beaches, seductively undulating palm trees and a few thousand hard-working, friendly, Christian, English-speaking natives. We would offer political stability, hemispheric solidarity with another British Commonwealth entity, the protection of our Armed Forces (we could commandeer two submarines from the West Edmonton Mall, if necessary) . . .

Oh yeah—and every year around the beginning of November, an invasion of approximately thirty million sun-starved, fishbelly-white, fellow-citizen tourists.

A no-brainer, right? Thirty tropical islands? Our nation's very own West Indian resort destination? William Seward paid $7 million to buy Alaska from Russia back in 1867. That worked out pretty well. We were being offered a tropical archipelago with in-house lobster—no icebergs, glaciers or blackflies—for free!

And our learned leaders passed. Incredibly, this was not the first time. Way back in 1917, Prime Minister Robert Borden proposed we annex the Turks and Caicos outright. His own government nixed the idea. In 1974 a brilliant, forward-thinking Ontario NDP Member of Parliament by the name of Max Saltsman introduced a bill proposing consolidation of the islands under the Canadian flag. His colleagues yawned and slumbered on. Even as late as 2004, MP Peter Goldring, representing the federal Tories, hopped a jet to the islands to explore the idea first-hand. He went, he saw, he presented his findings to a government committee. And then, nothing. Once again, a golden opportunity sank like a harpooned beluga.

The nabobs of negativism who scuttle the idea every time it bobs up have all kinds of nervous Nellie, quintessentially Canadian reasons. We'd have to amend the Canadian constitution, they say. It might offend other provinces and make them jealous, they claim. Besides, it's economically risky.

I say: Are You Nuts?

So what if we have to amend the constitution? We did it for Newfoundland in '49; we do it for Quebec about every six months.

Other provincial noses will be out of joint? Here's a thought: Get Over It.

Economically risky? Canadians leave behind billions of loonies each winter in the Caribbean, Mexico, Central America, Hawaii and the so-called Sunshine States. How bad could it be if we spent all that money in a place that collects and pays Canadian taxes?

Do the hacks, troughers and benchwarmers of Ottawa not realize that the political regime that actually succeeds in bringing to Canada a new piece of real estate where it never snows would be immortalized in poetic verse, adulatory prose and on the ten o'clock news for the Rest of Time?

Leonard Cohen would write a song about you. k.d. lang would sing it.

Stephen, Michael, Jack—could you just for once pull together on this one thing? For the greater Canadian good?

Gilles Duceppe? You could come on board too. We've already seen you in a hairnet. You'd be a knockout in a grass skirt.

IS YOUR SPARE CHANGE
SPYING ON YOU?

*Being slightly paranoid is like being slightly pregnant. It
tends to get worse.*

—MOLLY IVINS

One thing you've got to hand to the Americans: since 9/11, they've been hair-trigger alert to any cross-border security threats. Take the Great Canadian Quarter Plot of 2006. A damn close call, my friends.

What? You didn't hear about it? Well, you can thank your CBC—your Communist Broadcasting Corporation—for that.

What happened was, a group of US military contractors doing business (?) in Ottawa noticed a subtle but treacherous and continuing occurrence. Almost every time they bought a package of cigarettes, a beer or a magazine and got Canadian change, that change contained some highly suspicious coinage—to whit, one or two Canadian twenty-five cent pieces that had obviously been "tampered with."

These American contractors were sophisticated businessmen of the world. They weren't born yesterday. They recognized a wily and nefarious attempt by sinister foreign powers to undermine their mission and subvert America. The contractors collected the questionable quarters and delivered them, along with a report, to the US Department of Defense. In their report they noted that the coins were "anomalous" and "filled with something man-made that looked like nano-technology."

"It did not appear to be electronic (analog) in nature or to have a power source," the report noted. "Under a high power microscope, it appeared to be complex, consisting of several layers of clear, but different material, with a wire-like mesh suspended on top."

The contractors' conclusion: obviously the Canadian government was attempting to plant miniature radio transmitters on unsuspecting Sons of America.

Did the US Defense Department buy it? Hook, line and stinker. They issued an official espionage warning that the suspect coins "may contain embedded transmitters capable of eavesdropping." The Pentagon even launched an official investigation.

They could have saved themselves a lot of time and money by dropping one of those quarters in the coin slot of a public pay phone to make a call to the Canadian Mint.

They would have been told that the sinister twenty-five-cent pieces were in fact "poppy quarters"—commemorative coins issued on behalf of the Royal Canadian Legion to observe the sixtieth anniversary of the D-Day landings in Europe.

So it goes in the loony world of post 9/11 paranoia—and it ain't just our American cousins that are going gaga. Consider "Fortress Britain." Then-Prime Minister Gordon Brown recently announced a massive new anti-terrorism initiative that threatens to make "that green and gentle land" look like the inner circle of the Guantanamo Bay detention camp. Massive concrete "anti-blast" barriers are to be erected around some 250 UK train stations, as well as major shopping centres and movie theatres. Britishers booking tickets to travel abroad will be required to answer fifty-three personal questions—*from their travel agent.*

And for what? How many public places can you protect from some anonymous fanatic with a couple of sticks of dynamite stuffed under his mackintosh? As columnist Jenni Russell notes in the *Guardian,* "What good does it do to scan passengers at London's Kings Cross railway station if a bomber could still blow himself up in any market?" The government initiative, she writes, "does nothing to make us generally safer. All it does is make us feel that we're living in a new state: the state of terror."

Not to mention in the province of Dumb and Dumber. Last month, a restaurant called the Anchorage Inn caught fire in Rouses

Point, New York. Officials in the town of Lacolle, Quebec, only eight miles away, instantly dispatched a fire truck to aid their American neighbours.

Which they might have done, if US armed guards hadn't barred their way at the US border crossing. Reason? The Canadian fire-fighters had neglected to bring along their passports. Two other fire trucks behind them, with sirens blaring and lights flashing, were also stopped by the border guards.

Border integrity was secured. Alas, the restaurant burned to the ground.

Nobody said it better than Banksy, a famous British graffiti artist. His latest offering appears on a brick wall next to a police station in suburban London. It reads: "HELP! I NEED SOMEONE TO PROTECT ME FROM ALL THE MEASURES THEY TAKE IN ORDER TO PROTECT ME!"

It looks like Banksy will soon have lots more concrete on which to display his handiwork.

WHAT'S WITH THE ZOMBIES?

zombie: (zom-bee) noun. The body of a dead person given semblance of life, but mute and will-less, by a supernatural force, usually for some evil purpose.

Back in the Jurassic era, when dinosaurs browsed, pterodactyls soared and I was trying to grow a decent set of sideburns, I put in a stint as a bar boy in a nightclub in downtown Toronto. I learned a lot there, such as how to tell the difference between a quiet drunk and a mean one; how to carry a full tray of rye shots and beer chasers without spilling a drop; and . . . what the Jug was for.

The Jug lived under the bar out of sight of the customers. It was a big one, maybe twenty gallons, and it had a funnel jammed in its neck. One of my last jobs each night was to upend every supposedly empty bottle we had sold that day into the funnel. Beer, rum, wine, whiskey, absinthe, lemon gin, crème de cacao, sherry, port—all the dregs of every pint, mickey and twenty-sixer went down the funnel and into the jug. Sounds chintzy, but you'd be amazed at the gallon-age all those drips and drabs would add up to at the end of the day.

The resultant admixture was something to behold. Its colour varied from mud-brown to a sulphurous blue-green and sometimes it bubbled and smoked like a living thing. Even the fruit flies would have nothing to do with it.

Mostly the Jug just sat there fermenting evilly, but every once in a while a customer—a college kid, usually, or someone else profoundly green—would order a specific drink and one of the bartenders would swing into action. He would grab a tall glass, squirt in some pine-apple, orange and lime juice, perhaps a shot of cheap bar brandy, a spoonful of sugar, a fistful of ice and then . . .

He would siphon off about three ounces of the vile magma seething in the Jug and add it to the glass.

The drink was, of course, a Zombie. A truly horrid alcoholic concoction designed for the Not-Too-Bright, the Suicidal or those determined to lose their virginity no matter what the cost. It is called a Zombie because it renders the drinker near-catatonic. We topped our Zombies up with sludge from the Jug because we knew anyone idiotic enough to order a Zombie couldn't tell Mumm's Extra Dry from Mennen Aftershave.

All this preambling reverie to pose a question: what's with all the zombies these days? Google "zombies" and you get over twenty-one million hits—and that's without getting into zombie games, zombie songs, zombie movies, zombie wars—even zombie baseball.

We live in zombie times, I guess. Look at the world financial situation. It cratered, as we all remember, only to be resurrected with massive transfusions of supernatural plasma (read: taxpayers' dollars). And there it stands, tottering on the world stage, grunting and snorting incoherently. Our banks and money markets are being "run" once again by the same geniuses who took us over the cliff in the first place. Dead? Hell, no. Zombie bankers walk among us.

Down in the US, zombie Republicans thought to be dead and buried after the Obama victory have shoved back their tombstones to once again roil and heave across the landscape, muttering darkly of Kenyan passports, Marxist takeovers and (shudder) Canadian medicine.

And here at home? We have our ongoing engagement in Afghanistan, the zombie war that won't lie down. We have a zombie deficit, a zombie health care crisis and I haven't even mentioned the Toronto Maple Leafs (zombies on skates—the horror, the horror).

And then we have our leaders: Stephen "Our-Lady-of-Perpetual-Minority" Harper; Michael "the Undead" Ignatieff, survivor of more knives in the back than a beef brisket at Swiss Chalet; and Jack Layton, standing firm in the polls at 15 percent. And still unaccountably breathing.

The Irish mystic W.B. Yeats was ahead of us all. Nearly a century ago he wrote a poem called "The Second Coming." It prophesied the appearance of a man-like creature with "a gaze blank and pitiless as the sun" stirring in the sands of the desert.

The poem asks:

And what rough beast, its hour come round at last,
Slouches towards Bethlehem to be born?

My money's on a zombie.

PART FOUR

SAY IT, WITH FEELINGS

A-HUNTING WE WILL GO

They call hunting and fishing "game." It's the only game
where the other team never volunteered to play.

—MATT NORTH

So these two brothers, good ol' boys, are creeping along in their pickup, headlights off, down a rural back road outside Owen Sound, Ontario, just after sundown. They're driving slow, peering intently into woodlots and brush piles on both sides of the road. Finally the driver sees what they're looking for. He cuts the ignition, coasts to a stop, nods wordlessly toward a thicket of scrub willow.

White-tailed buck. Three-pointer. Silhouetted against the horizon. The brother in the passenger seat rolls down his window, hauls out a high-powered hunting rifle from behind the seat and draws a bead. No need to hurry. The deer just stands there like a statue.

BLAM! BLAM! The deer is still standing there like a statue. BLAM!

That's because it is a statue. A decoy. Two conservation officers materialize by the pickup and the brothers are busted for poaching.

Hunting from a car: redneck couch potato heaven. Almost as much fun as fishing with dynamite.

I'd like to tell you the judge threw the book at them, but the brothers found themselves a slithery lawyer who argued that using a decoy deer to tantalize his clients amounted to entrapment. The case has dragged on through two appeals and three years of litigation and shows no sign of resolution anytime soon.

If there's a glint of gold in this judicial mare's nest, perhaps it's the fact that animals—even ersatz ones—are finally getting their day in court. But change has been coming for some time. Don't forget just a few generations ago, English bluebloods thought it great sport to put a bear in a pit and unleash a pack of hunting dogs to worry it to death.

Jim West might have a tough time believing that. He's a recreational hunter who lives up near 70 Mile House in British Columbia. West was out with his dogs scouting for moose one day when a hunter's worst nightmare came thundering down on him. He got himself between a bear cub and a very angry momma grizzly. She swatted him sprawling, not once but twice. West grabbed a tree limb and swatted back. He managed to stun the bear and then kill it with the tree limb. West stumbled back to his vehicle and drove himself to a hospital. The cuts in his scalp, arms and face took sixty stitches to close. He was lucky to be alive. Then his real troubles started.

Word of his encounter hit the media—along with the news that conservation officers had tracked down and destroyed two bear cubs the mother bear had been protecting. Animal rights crusaders ignited a firestorm of protest. West's phone began to ring around the clock. A blizzard of emails hit media outlets across the province. One zealot went so far as to impersonate Jim West, sending out a fake email in West's name claiming that actually, his dogs had started the whole thing by chasing the bears up a tree.

One woman accosted West and asked him why he hadn't "just run away" when he saw the bear. I doubt that West would have got very far. I've been told that in a hundred-yard dash, a grizzly can outrun a horse. Jim West agrees. "You can't outrun a mother bear," he says.

A lot of folks get a tad dotty when it comes to our relations with animals—few more so than Jennifer Thornburg of North Carolina.

Excuse me—that should be Cut-out Dissection.com of North Carolina. Ms., er, Cut-out Dissection, had her name legally changed to publicize the plight of animals that wind up as specimens in high school biology classes. She acknowledges that her new moniker can be a bit of a pain. "I normally do have to repeat my name several times when I am introducing myself," she says. But it's a price she's willing to pay on behalf of the suffering animals.

Yeah, well . . .

Loony-tunes like Ms. Cut-out Dissection.com aside, perhaps we actually have hauled ourselves a rung or so higher on the evolutionary ladder. Maybe we've outgrown the notion that we can treat the rest of the natural world as our personal amusement park-cum-petting/shooting zoo. If so, Lady Margot Asquith was way ahead of her time. The British socialite and wife of an earl lived when bear-baiting was still legal and riding to the hounds was all the rage. At a ball, she overheard someone extolling the remarkable jumping prowess of various fox-harrying horsemen. "Jump?" sniffed Lady Asquith, "Anyone can jump. Look at fleas."

GETTING YOUR MONEY'S WORTH

Bank: a place that lends you money if you can prove you don't need it.

—Bob Hope

Banker: someone who lends you an umbrella when the sun is shining, then wants it back when it starts to rain.

—Mark Twain

Ah, yes . . . the banking institution. Is there any other business calling that so inspires our contempt? Well, Colombian drug lords, maybe—but at least drug dealers have the decency to get shot, stabbed, strangled or stomped to death by their rivals once in a while. Bankers rake in the same kind of profits without ever besmirching their French cuffs.

Take Gord Nixon, CEO of the Royal Bank. I don't know how Gord's making ends meet lately, but the figures are in for 2006 and that was a rather good year for Gord. He pulled down just a little under $13 million for his efforts in that twelve-month period. He must have worked extra hard. He only made $10.3 million the year before.

Mind you, it's not as if Gord was swiping money from the till. Royal Bank made a grotesquely bloated profit of $4.7 billion in 2006. You read right—four point seven.

With a "b."

It is temptingly easy to dismiss bankers as twenty-first-century

pirates in pinstripes—the James-Younger Gang without the charisma—but that wouldn't explain State Bank & Trust in Fargo, North
Dakota.

Oh, State Bank & Trust makes money hand over fist too. But
then . . . something unusual happens.

One December, for instance, each and every employee at the
bank—and there are five hundred people who work there—got a
Christmas bonus of $1,000.

But it's a bank, right? So naturally, there was a catch—some "fine
print," as it were.

The employees weren't allowed to take their free grand and go out
and blow it on a five-star restaurant, a shop-til-you-drop blitzkrieg at
the local mall or a down payment on a tank of regular unleaded for
the family Chevy. No. Nor could they just, er, put the money in the
bank. They had to unload it.

"There are three rules," explained Michael Solberg, State Bank's
chief operating officer. "You can't give it to your family. You can't
give it to a co-worker. And you have to document your deed. Other
than that, the sky's the limit."

Quite a challenge. And one that the Fargo State Bank employees
rose to admirably. One teller paid his thousand dollars to a North
Dakota veterinary surgeon who performed a life-saving operation on
an abandoned, dying kitten. Another employee went out and bought
enough DVDs and DVD players to outfit patients in a local cancer
ward.

Having a thousand bucks to play with isn't exactly like winning
the Joker's Wild lottery but, judiciously applied, it's enough of a cash
transfusion to put someone's temporarily hijacked life back on the
rails. One bank worker turned his money over to a friend whose car
had just been stolen. Another donated it to a young, recently wid-
owed woman who was struggling to make mortgage payments and to
cover her husband's funeral bills.

In short, the money was applied five hundred different ways,
bringing unexpectedly happy endings to five hundred different, difficult situations.

And that was just the beginning.

The various good deeds the employees did with their relayed nest
eggs rebounded back on them. Turned out that by physically giving

it away, they made themselves happier, too—much more than simply writing a cheque to a charity would have. One employee explained, "You actually, truly see the benefit better by doing it yourself." And it becomes personal. A bank secretary said, "[The money] actually gets to the people that we know in the community who need it."

But I think another State Bank & Trust employee said it best. When a reporter asked one of the clerks what she and her colleagues got out of the exercise, she replied: "Just a real good feeling of giving."

That's something that Gord Nixon can't buy. Not even with $12.8 million.

TWO FEET EQUALS
SIX FEET UNDER

Do you, like me, have a soft spot for modern fairy tales? *The Cement-filled Cadillac*? *The Choking Doberman*? The first one is a tale of just deserts for a rich guy caught fooling around with the wife of a cement-truck driver. *The Choking Doberman*? It's about a family watchdog found to have a throat obstruction—three human fingers belonging to a burglar still cowering in a bedroom cupboard.

Urban legends—morality tales just a little too vindictively satisfying to be true.

Here's another one you can add to the list: *Cement Shoes*.

You know how this one goes. Cement shoes are the grisly fate of, say, Machete Joe Maniago, a low-browed gunsel who worked for the Mob as an enforcer until he got caught skimming from his weekly "collections."

Police investigators would later piece together the grisly details of his demise. How he was ambushed in the parking lot of a strip club, thrown into the trunk of a Lincoln and driven to a remote shack in the Jersey Pine Barrens. There, he would have been tied to a chair, tongue-lashed and pistol-whipped. Finally, his interrogator would have smiled and said, "Okay, Joe, now kick off your Guccis."

Machete Joe would have watched with eyes as big as hard-boiled eggs as his feet were immersed in a tub of cement. Joe knew what came next. A quick trip through the night to a small boat moored to a deserted pier. A short ride out to the middle of the river or the ocean offshore and then . . . over the side with Joe. Cement shoes, an impossibly horrible fate.

Except . . . not.

Well, think about it. Hit men—even sadistic ones—are time management specialists at heart. They know murder is exceedingly illegal, to be got over with as quickly as possible. You think they're going to kidnap a guy, drop the hammer—and then *sit around for an hour or two waiting for some cement to dry?*

And then there's the weight factor. Pasta lover that he was, chances are better than average that Machete Joe was already a bit of a porker. You think the hit squad would want to add another hundred pounds or so of Portland cement to their burden?

As Paulie Walnuts would (approximately) say: "It don't make no freakin' sense."

Indeed it doesn't. And although the plot device of throwing someone into the drink with their feet encased in cement has proved extremely hardy with underworld gossips, nightclub comics, crime novelists and television producers, an examination of criminal records reveals that exactly zero bodies, or remains of bodies, have ever been recovered anywhere that were dipped in tubs of cement.

This is not to say that certain parties have not been weighed down with heavy objects and turned into involuntary sea bottom attractions. Various corpses have been found wired to cinder blocks or with heavy objects in their pockets. Racketeer Johnnie "Chink" Goodman was fished out of a stream in New Jersey back in 1941, closely involved with a big block of concrete—but his body was chained to the ballast, not immersed in it. That negates the entire grisly charm of the cement shoes.

Nevertheless, personal experience compels me to confirm that the Cement Shoe concept can be extremely effective as an agent for public change. I offer you the case of Larry W., a fellow in our community well known for climbing aboard various bandwagons. A few years back, Larry got his picture on the front page of our local newspaper. The photograph showed Larry sitting on a chair, sledgehammer by his side, dressed in Bermuda shorts with his legs clearly immersed in a washtub of hardened cement. Larry, the newspaper copy informed us, had vowed not to smash his way out of the cement until . . .

I forget what particular issue Larry was protesting that day, but he vowed his feet would remain encased in the cement until the issue was favourably resolved.

That same afternoon I ran into Larry at the pub. He was barefoot (not all that unusual for Larry), languidly sipping a beer. "Larry," I said, "you won your protest already?"

"Not at all, boy," said Larry. "I just got thirsty."

And that's when I recalled that Larry had been wearing gumboots in the newspaper photo. Gumboots that he could slip out of any time he pleased, cement or no cement.

Moral of this urban legend: if anyone ever offers to outfit you with cement shoes, remember to request gumboots.

IT'S HOW YOU PLAY THE GAME

"If a tie is like kissing your sister, losing is like kissing your grandmother with her teeth out."

—GEORGE BRETT

Poor old George. He was a great baseball player and an occasionally funny guy, but he just didn't get it. Life really isn't just about winning or losing.

Lots of other famous folks whose names begin with "B" have figured that out—Bono, Warren Buffet, Brangelina and Bill (as in Gates). What do they have in common? They all had tons of dough and they all gave tons of it away.

If you hope to croak with a smile on your face, it's the second part of the last sentence that really matters. There is no real joy in Getting Stuff—and that grim truth applies equally to billionaires and bag ladies. Whether you're piling up coffers of krugerrands or shopping carts full of plastic bags, a simple truth applies: a human being can only use so much crap in a lifetime.

The real happiness comes from giving it away—there's even scientific proof of that. Researchers at the University of British Columbia targeted a group of youths and "gifted" them with cash. Half the group got to keep the money; the other half was directed to pass it along to others. The second group reported significantly higher feelings of satisfaction and happiness than the first.

A follow-up survey of six hundred adults showed that rates of happiness increased proportionally with the amount of money people gave away, not the amount they had earned or spent on themselves.

There is however, another "B" word that effectively cuts a lot of us potential players out of the philanthropy game. That word is "broke." Most of us can't indulge in the Generosity Sweepstakes because we're, ahem, lacking in financial fluidity. Skint. Busted.

Well, there's good news for us, too. Turns out you don't need to hand out cash to feel good. Paying compliments is just as rewarding as doling out dollars.

Japanese researchers at the National Institute for Physiological Sciences in Okazaki employed a brain-scanning technique known as functional magnetic resonance imaging to track a group of nineteen healthy people through a series of experiments. It was a complicated set-up, but basically it confirmed that the human brain does not discriminate between material and immaterial rewards. "We found that different kinds of rewards—a good reputation versus money—are biologically coded by the same neural structure, the striatum," said Dr. Norihiro Sadato, chief researcher.

Simply put, as far as your brain is concerned, praise is just as good as cash.

So is simple kindness. And kindness comes from a well that never goes dry—providing you prime it.

A couple of years ago there was a baseball game at Western Oregon University that would have made George Brett smile, if not laugh out loud. The Western women's softball team was playing a crew from Central Washington and Sara Tucholsky was in the batter's box. She took a couple of strikes and then caught a sweet pitch that came right over the plate, belt-high. She swung. She connected. The ball sailed up, up and over the centre field fence. Sara was ecstatic. It was her first home run ever. She started to run the bases, but in her excitement she failed to touch first. Her teammates shouted, she lurched to a stop on the baseline so harshly that her legs buckled and she fell to the ground. She tore a ligament. She couldn't walk at all.

Baseball rules are very straightforward. If Sara Tucholsky couldn't make it around the bases then the home run was cancelled. Under the rules her teammates were forbidden to help her. Tough. But rules are rules.

Unless . . .

Mallory Holtman, the pitcher for Central Washington, approached the umpire. What if the injured batter was carried around the bases *by members of the opposing team?*

Nothing in the rule book about that.

The pitcher and the shortstop from the other side picked Sara up and carried her around all the bases. The action cost the Central Washington team the game. When they touched home plate Sara was crying, but not from a sore knee. "They didn't even know it was my first home run," she said. "It just says a lot about them."

Indeed it does. George Brett, please copy.

QUIT KVETCHING, START LIVING

Kvetch (Yiddish): to complain persistently about everything.

Henry Perowne is standing naked before a mirror. You'd never guess that he is a successful British neurosurgeon in the prime of life, healthy, with two successful, grown children. There's no way to discern from his fit but middle-aged body that he lives in a splendid heritage townhouse in downtown London, drives a Jaguar, plays squash, loves classical music.

But naked Henry Perowne is not reflecting on any of that. He is thinking about hot water.

Henry Perowne is the main character in Ian McEwan's best selling novel, *Saturday*. Here is what Henry Perowne is thinking as he steps into the shower and turns on the tap:

When this civilization falls, when the Romans, whoever they are this time round, have finally left and the new Dark Age begins, this will be one of the first luxuries to go. The old folk crouching by their peat fires will tell their disbelieving grandchildren of standing naked mid-winter under jet streams of hot clean water.

Hot clean water. Everyone reading these words has had access to it pretty much every day of their lives. When's the last time any of us—aside from Ian McEwan—recognized the simple miracle of that?

We need to cultivate, as the cliché goes, an attitude of gratitude. And here's the ironic kicker: thanks to the Big Bubble Burst—to the layoffs, shutdowns, downturns, the pancaking investment portfolios and the scorched earth real estate debacle—thanks to all the recent Bad News it looks like people are . . . becoming more grateful.

For sure there's a lot less whining going on. There aren't many of us who haven't been adversely affected in some way by the Big Bubble Burst. It has sideswiped us all, reminding us that there's more to life than Big Macs, Walmart specials and Britney Spears knickers or lack thereof. We have all been reminded that life, at bottom, is not frivolous. It is serious. And that reminder, in a paradoxical way, seems to be making us more content.

Take purple bracelets. You may have seen someone wearing one. If you haven't you probably will soon. Some six million North Americans sport purple bracelets on their wrists already and the number is growing faster than the bankruptcy rate.

Purple bracelets are the brainwave of a Protestant minister, Will Bowen of Kansas City, Missouri. He runs a non-profit called A Complaint Free World, Inc., the mission of which is simple: to encourage people to quit bitching and start living. Thus the purple bracelets. Reverend Bowen challenges wearers to switch the bracelet from one wrist to the other every time they complain about something. The goal is to go twenty-one days without switching.

By the time you manage that, chances are your outlook on life will be a whole lot sunnier.

The Reverend Bowen has offered his bracelet as a handy daily talisman against the rough patch the world is currently weathering. He figures an adjustment in attitude is as good as a course correction. "In good times," he told a *Wall Street Journal* reporter, "people often take for granted what they have and whine about what they don't have. Bad times make people more grateful."

Me, I'm not crazy about the idea of wearing more jewellery, purple or otherwise—but I admire the concept. Here's what I recommend.

Start your day off like Henry Perowne—naked, in front of the bathroom mirror. Now instead of moaning about the crow tracks around your eyes, the love handles amidships or the, as Leonard Cohen puts it, "aches in the places where you used to play"—instead of all the petty junk, enlist in my Two Step Recovery Program.

Step One: Conjure up three simple things in your everyday life for which you can be grateful.

Could be little stuff—your nice smile, the robins chirping in the lilac by the bathroom window, the smell of coffee brewing in the kitchen. Could be big stuff—your kids, the roof over your head, the air in your lungs.

Step Two: Be thankful.

And if you're still feeling sorry for yourself, step into the shower and turn on the hot water tap.

MONEY: THE RUE OF ALL EVIL

*Money brings some happiness, but after a certain point,
it just brings more money.*

—NEIL SIMON

Jefri Bolkiah is a chap who could shout "Amen" to that. Jefri is a fellow who knows a thing or two about money—not that you'd ever guess as much if you met him. Jefri wears a perpetual frown and peers out at the world through a pair of furtive, backward-glancing eyes, like a kid caught with his hand in the cookie jar.

Strange behaviour, considering that he's not exactly without resources. It's "Prince" Jefri, for starters. His brother is the Sultan of Brunei, which is to say, one of the wealthiest men on the planet.

The sultan may control the purse strings but little bro Jefri has been making do nicely with hand-me-downs. He has a personal fleet of 1,700—yes, you read right—luxury cars. He also maintains a 180-foot yacht and owns hundreds of paintings by Picasso, Renoir, Modigliani and the like. And for those oh-so important getaways, he has his very own New York *pied-à-terre*—the Palace Hotel.

All of it.

But that's all about to morph into the past tense. Prince Jefri, in his capacity as head of Brunei's investment agency, has made rather a bollocks of the business. He's managed in just a few short years to blow a total of $14.8 billion US.

How? No one's more mystified than Prince Jefri. "I keep asking the lawyers," says the prince. "Where did it go?"

Here's a suggestion, Jefri: frisk those lawyers before you let them out of the room.

As penance, Prince Jefri has agreed to turn over what's left of his assets—the yacht, the hotel, the paintings and the 1,700 cars—to his older, smarter brother. He just hopes the sultan is feeling benevolent enough to leave him some scraps—say, a few dozen limos and a couple of floors of the Palace, perhaps a Picasso engraving or two—to eke out some wretched kind of hand-to-mouth existence.

Takes all kinds. Kinds like George Whitman, for instance. George couldn't be less like Prince Jefri. Nary a limo nor luxury yacht to his name, and certainly no connections to royalty. George lives in Paris where he skippers a run-down bookstore called Shakespeare and Company on the Left Bank opposite Notre Dame cathedral. He's been doing the same thing since 1951 and he's got about as much dough in the bank as he had when he started out, which is to say, *rien*.

Could be his business acumen. When it comes to turning a buck, George isn't exactly Donald Trump. His motto: "Give what you can; take what you need."

That's the philosophy George Whitman has operated under for the past six decades. He also offers a free place to bunk for anybody in need for as long as they need.

(Well, almost free. George expects freeloaders to help out around the shop.) The bookshop now boasts a dozen beds. George reckons that over the years, some forty thousand people have spent at least one night at Shakespeare and Company. The guest list has included Allen Ginsberg, Henry Miller, Richard Wright and William Burroughs.

George doesn't do the heavy lifting around Shakespeare and Company anymore—his daughter Sylvia has taken over. But the old man is still there, every day, smiling and sipping his iced tea from a chipped water glass as he oversees his "tumbleweeds," as he calls his just-passing-through staff, making sure they don't screw up the business.

So. Two men, one of them richer than most of us can imagine; the other a nonagenarian without, as the saying approximately goes, an urn to urinate in.

One guy is happy as a clam; the other is going nuts with worry.

Conclusions? Draw your own. But I would point out that a couple of years ago, the British Broadcasting Corporation took it upon itself to discover "the happiest place on earth." They investigated the fleshpots of America and the cultural pearls of Europe and the Middle East. They also checked out the socialist Edens of Norway and Denmark, which placed surprisingly high.

But they settled on Pentecost, one of eighty-three islands that make up the nation of Vanuatu, in the South Pacific. The GNP of Pentecost is non-existent. The citizens don't even have money. What they have is an abiding sense of community, which, the BBC investigative team concluded, is the most important prerequisite for happiness of all.

So appreciate your neighbours. Rejoice that our greedy, grasping world can still make room for a George Whitmore . . .

And spare a kind thought for poor Prince Jefri of Brunei.

TOO DUMB TO COME IN
OUT OF THE RAIN

*Men are stupid and women are crazy. And the reason
women are so crazy is because men are so stupid.*
                                    —GEORGE CARLIN

Over the last dozen years 648 Americans have been flash barbecued into the afterworld by lightning strikes. An astounding 524
of them—more than 80 percent—had one factor (aside from citizen-
ship) in common. Care to guess?

Pockets full of iron filings, perhaps? Horseshoes in their fedoras
you think? A big sign reading "God Is Dead" Scotch-taped to their
backsides?

Nope—what they had in common was gender. More than eight
out of every ten Americans struck and killed by lightning were men.
Some of them were fishing; others were out on the golf course or playing baseball. Some were just mowing the lawn.

Scientists have been mulling over this mystery for a few years
now. Just what is it that causes lightning to single out such a prepon-
derance of men over women for fatal strikes? Some deep thinkers
thought it might be a variation on the "tall poppy syndrome"—men
being statistically taller than women would theoretically make them
better conductors of electricity, but no, analysis showed that the men
who died weren't particularly tall. Others wondered if there might be
some electromagnetic component in testosterone that was attracting
those lightning bolts.

Then somebody said, "Maybe we should study women to see if they have some genetic condition that protects them from fatal lightning strikes."

Turns out they do. Far fewer women are killed by lightning because when the skies start to grumble women who find themselves outdoors instinctively respond to a primordial, inbred reflex.

They seek shelter.

You won't find many women casting for trout, driving a golf ball or shagging pop flies in a thunderstorm because, to put it bluntly, such behaviour is dumb.

Men? Well . . .

"Men take more risks in lightning storms," says John Jensenius of the US National Weather Service. Why? Good question. Could be that men, too, are responding to a primordial instinct. Call it the John Wayne reflex—the one that says a man should always appear macho and fearsome when danger lurks.

Even when it's just plain stupid.

So far it's just a theory, but it goes a long way toward explaining phenomena like professional wrestling, barroom head-butting contests and the continuing adulation of Don Cherry.

Not to mention the behaviour of those two macaroons who, in October 2009, thought it would be a good idea to sneak into the Siberian tiger enclosure at the Calgary Zoo in the middle of the night.

No doubt the tiger thought it was a good idea too. It was his first taste of free-range cretin.

The two intruders were lucky to escape with a mauling, but I doubt their luck will hold. Those guys are two lightning strikes waiting to happen.

Which brings us to Steve Melvin of Madison, Ohio. Steve not only stays out in lightning storms, he's willing to drive hundreds of miles to do it. Steve is a "storm chaser"—a guy who gets his jollies by driving into thunderstorms, getting out of the car and taking photos. In June 1989, Steve got his near-death wish—he was struck by a bolt of lightning.

Or rather his camera was. The lightning melted the camera right down the front of the tripod, but somehow the film inside was not destroyed. When it was developed, Steve claims that the final exposure on the film shows the ghostly outline of a human figure framed in the lightning flash.

It couldn't be Steve—he was behind the camera.

"I've heard all the guesses," says Steve. "Some say it was me having an out-of-body experience; others say it was something from a whole different dimension. My wife says it looks like my grandmother come down from heaven."

I'd go with the grandmother explanation, Steve. And I bet if you could hear her, she'd be saying, "Get your butt indoors, you idiot!"

ALL THE RAGE

Do not go gentle into that good night
Rage, rage, against the dying of the light
—DYLAN THOMAS

Ah, if only the magnificent Welsh loon could be living among us at this hour. Alas, that cannot be. Mr. Thomas hiccupped off his mortal coil way back in 1953, not too long after enthusiastically downing eighteen successive shots of whisky in a New York saloon.

A drunken rage, to be sure, but a rage nonetheless. Dylan Thomas would probably be amused to learn that more than a half a century later many of us still rage, rage against the dying of the light, although nowadays it's more likely to be a green light dying and morphing into a yellow that gets us foaming at the mouth. *Damn! Stuck at the intersection again! Pound the dashboard! Hammer the horn with your fist! Swear like a tar sands roughneck while you glare at the back of the head of the driver in the car in front of you!*

Road Rage, in all its ugly manifestations, is all the, er, rage.

But a human being with an urge to vent has a cornucopia of options these days. Cattle car conditions and assorted in-flight indignities in the air travel business have given rise to a phenomenon known as Air Rage, in which seemingly Caspar Milquetoastish customers suddenly morph into crazed berserkers.

Recently three do-gooder passengers on British Airways flight 2237 had to tackle, pin down and help handcuff a fellow air traveller who had headbutted the passenger beside him, indecently assaulted a flight attendant and threatened to strangle the pilot.

All of this at thirty-five thousand feet somewhere over the Atlantic between Gatwick and Orlando.

But you don't have to fly commercial to fly off the handle. Another avenue is Checkout Line Rage. Chances are you've suffered a touch of this yourself, standing in a lineup at the cash register with an armload of veggies and toilet paper and a brick of pralines and cream slowly liquefying in your arms while some maroon three places in front of you tries to amalgamate his street address, his wife's birthday and his pickup truck licence plate into a "lucky" lottery ticket number.

Then there's that old cyberspace standby, Computer or Web Rage. This refers to brain-frying tantrums sparked by the infuriating antics of your laptop—glacial-speed downloads, links to nowhere and crazy-making on-screen pronouncements such as: "This program has performed an illegal function and will be shut down."

We are of course familiar with Work Rage—those increasingly common outbreaks of spontaneous mayhem erupting in offices, factories and other formerly pacific workspaces. Sometimes it's just shouting or kicking a wastebasket; other times it involves intimidation and even physical confrontations between colleagues.

Post office workers seem to be particularly susceptible to this malaise—so much so that when any wage earner puts down his ballpoint and picks up an assault rifle, we call it "going postal."

Far be it from me to dump on my fellow testosteronians, but have you ever noticed how it's almost always *guys* who go nuts behind the wheel, in the air, over the Xerox machine or at the supermarket checkout counter? Women hardly ever go bananas in public. There's a physiological explanation for that too. Doctors call it IMS—Irritable Male Syndrome. Ironic, because this bull-in-a-china-shop behaviour is caused not by an excess of "bullishness," but by a lack of it. Men suffering from IMS exhibit anger and irritability because of depleted testosterone levels.

Chemically induced or not, social rage is kicking out the jambs in all directions. Observers have noted an emerging syndrome they call Prevenge—violent action taken *in anticipation* of a harmful action.

A kind of pre-rage rage, if you will.

Where will it end? Perhaps in a state that Briton Luke Birmingham describes as Rage Rage—a condition that affects people who rage against people who commit road rage, work rage, air rage, etcetera.

Sounds a little out-rage-ous to me—but I've got a hunch that Dylan Thomas would understand. With or without the eighteen whiskies.

SMILE! IT'S GOOD FOR YOU!

Here's a fun experiment: draw a human face. Nothing fancy—just take a pencil and draw a circle on a piece of paper. Now add two dots for the eyes. Draw a smaller blob below them for the nose.

Doesn't tell you much of anything so far, right? Your subject could be loon-like hysterical or wrist-slashing suicidal. Ticked off or blissed out. There are no clues in that half-finished face.

Now take your pencil and draw a line for the mouth. Presto, you've got attitude.

If you draw the mouth like a hammock with the corners riding high, you've got a happy camper. Invert it and you've created Gloomy Gus.

All with one simple line.

At about this point you are saying approximately, "Yeah, so? It's a dumb cartoon. What's this got to do with real life?"

Everything. You want to elevate your mood and feel better—right this minute? Forget pills. Forget the double Drambuie. You don't need a hit from the Comedy Network.

All you have to do is lift the corners of your mouth and smile.

Fake it if you have to. Take that pencil you drew the face with and stick it crossways in your mouth. It works. In 1983, researchers at the University of Washington instructed half a dozen subjects to jam a pencil between their teeth, then showed them a series of cartoons.

They showed the same cartoons to six subjects who weren't required to "smile."

The pencil-clenchers rated the cartoons "significantly funnier" than the control group did.

It's powerful medicine, the smile. So powerful that it's common to cultures around the world, primitive and sophisticated alike. People everywhere smile when they're happy and frown when they're not. Charles Darwin, on his voyages aboard the *Beagle*, remarked on this cross-cultural phenomenon nearly two hundred years ago.

Best of all, the Smile is aide-de-camp to the Laugh, which is even more powerful medicine. Researchers at the University of Maryland Medical Center have been analyzing the therapeutic clout of simple laughter. They came to the conclusion that laughing:

- increases blood flow through the arteries;
- lowers blood sugar levels among diabetics,
- eases pain (because it relaxes muscles);
- regulates the immune system; and . . .
- even burns calories.

Wait a minute. You can *lose weight* by laughing?

Absolutely. Researchers at Vanderbilt University calculate that fifteen minutes of hearty laughter burns about forty calories. Do it every day and you'll drop four pounds over the next year.

And you thought watching the Parliamentary Channel was a waste of time.

Is there a downside to laughter? Not really. "A tranquilizer with no side effects," Arnold Glasow called it. Laughter is also an unparalleled tool of diplomacy. It is very hard to be angry with someone while you're laughing at them. At the same time it's an incredibly powerful skewering device to wield against your enemies. Adversaries can steel themselves for sneers, curses, growls, snarls, slanders and all manner of verbal abuse. But someone laughing at them? There's no defence against that.

And it starts with a smile. A simple flex of the lip muscles. Smile enough and your enemies will melt away before you have to bring out the heavy ordinance. At worst, you'll confound them on the spot. Or even longer. Lisa Gherardini's smile has been confounding viewers for more than five hundred years. Lisa Gherardini? Wife of a sixteenth-century Florentine silk merchant. We'd never have heard of her if her smile hadn't caught the eye of an artist named da Vinci about the time another young Italian named Columbus was setting sail from Spain to see what was over the horizon.

So smile. Worked for Mona Lisa. It'll work for you.

HOW LAZY CAN WE GET?

Oh, Beulah . . . peel me a grape.
—MAE WEST IN *I'M NO ANGEL*

At least Mae showed some pizzazz in her monumental laziness, appealing to her maid for masticatory assistance with the fruit plate. Three-quarters of a century after she uttered that line, we've lost her sense of style—but we're easily as bone lazy as Mae on her most slothful day. Consider Fake Mud.

Got yourself a Hummer-sized SUV but just can't find the time to get out and tear up a mountainside or crash through a bog the way they do in the TV ads? Not to worry. For fifteen bucks you can buy an aerosol can of gen-yew-wine Spray-on Mud. All you have to do is lather up your fenders, maybe a spritz or two on the windshield and you'll convince folks you spent the weekend up to your axles in primordial goo.

But maybe you're not the macho motorhead type. Perhaps you're a sun bunny whose idea of a good time is stretching out on a beach blanket to baste like a bratwurst. That, too, can be demanding. It's all very well to lie supine in the sun, slowly fricasseeing your skin cells to a golden brown, but how do you know when it's time to—you know—turn over?

Fear not! The Tan-Timer Bikini is the garment for you. A British manufacturer has come up with a two-piece that sports a built-in buzzer. It goes off every fifteen minutes to remind you to turn over to your unbaked side. Sort of like the guy who puts popcorn in his pancakes so they'll flip themselves.

Still too adventurous for you? Hey, even beer-guzzling sofa taters deserve a technological break. That's where Matthias Hahnen's Smart Beer Mat comes in. Matthias, a German inventor, and his beer drinking pal Robert Doerr put their hop-happy heads together and came up with an electronic device small and flat enough to fit under the standard cardboard beer mat. Minimal though it is, the gizmo uses weight and motion sensors to detect when the beer glass it's sitting under is nearly empty. When that critical stage is reached, the device emits a radio signal that is picked up by a receiver at the bar, notifying the bartender that there's a customer in need of a refill.

I tell ya, life is just getting simpler and simpler. Take shopping. You know how exhausting and stressful it can be, thrashing your way through the wilds of the fruit and vegetable section, trying to decide whether the Bosc pears are truly juicy or the avocados are actually edible. All that manual squeezing and prodding—it's exhausting!

Well, it used to be. Now, thanks to ripeSense Ltd., such experiences will shortly be a thing of the past. RipeSense has come up with an agricultural variation on the US Homeland Security colour-coded Threat Level System. It's a label that affixes to fruits and vegetables and turns colour as the fruit ripens. Red indicates firm, orange is crisp and yellow means juicy.

According to a company spokesperson, the label works by reacting to the ethylene gas that fruit emits as it ripens. "The label senses the 'aroma,' as you would smell the difference with your nose as a pear ripens," explains company representative Katie McInness.

Oh, yeah . . . noses. I remember when we used those things.

There are so many technological innovations to help us handle the tricky chore of feeding our faces that a body could get confused by all the options and maybe make a bad nutritional choice. Fortunately we have a Canadian invention that will take care of that for you. All you need is a cellphone with a video component and you're good to go. Subscribers to MyFoodPhone (it only costs about a hundred bucks a month) can send photographs of the meal they are about to eat to the company, where an on-line dietician will monitor the food for portion size and nutritional content.

Why, it's getting so that science will do everything but chew your food for you.

Actually, they're working on that too. Check out the latest product from a company called Hovis, Britain's most famous bread manufacturer.

It's called "Hovis Invisible Crust"—the world's first crustless loaf, produced especially for the 35 percent of British mothers who say they just can't persuade their children to take on the arduous task of chewing through crust to get at the bread.

Perhaps that explains British guitar great Eric Clapton's philosophy. He said: "Given the choice between accomplishing something and just loafing around, I'd rather just loaf around. No contest."

With a loaf of Hovis Invisible Crust no doubt. And Missus Clapton peeling grapes.

HEY, BUDDY . . .
FORGET SOMETHING?

You ever leave anything behind in a taxi? I swear the cab companies must install "stuff magnets" under the back seat to suck your personal effects right out of your pockets. I don't take cabs any more than I have to, but I've still left behind enough loot to outfit a Salvation Army thrift outlet. You name it—books, magazines, ballpoint pens, groceries, a harmonica or two and once, a bag of dirty laundry.

Naturally, I never saw any of it again (and I'm not holding my breath on the dirty laundry—although possibly the cab driver is).

I'm unusually gifted when it comes to leaving my property behind in taxis, but I'm not as good as Philippe Quint. Mr. Quint is a New York musician, and a very talented one, to boot. Talented enough to give a one-man concert in Dallas, Texas, not long ago. On his return to Manhattan he flagged a cab at the airport, took it to his apartment, paid the cabbie and retrieved his overnight bag from the trunk. As the taxi pulled away and Mr. Quint fumbled with his front door keys, something was gnawing at him. He felt . . . lacking. Unfulfilled. As if he'd forgotten something.

Indeed he had. In his haste, Mr. Quint had left his violin in the backseat of the taxi.

Actually it wasn't *his* violin. It belonged to two benefactors who had loaned it to Mr. Quint for his concert.

And the violin he'd left in the taxi wasn't a Japanese knock-off. It was one of only seven hundred or so handcrafted by an Italian gentleman some three centuries ago.

The violin Mr. Quint had left in the taxi was a Stradivarius.

The violin Mr. Quint had left in the taxi was worth

Four

Million

Dollars.

Mister Quint did the only thing a person can do when they have inadvertently left an object worth $4 million in the back of a taxi that has disappeared and they can't even remember which bloody taxi company it was. He sat down on the sidewalk and cried.

And then he sprang into action. Yellow Cab! He remembered that it was a Yellow Cab from Newark that he'd been in. He phoned the head office. Naw, no fiddle's been turned in here, pal. Hours went by. Philippe Quint considered changing his name, moving to Tanganyika, jumping out the window . . .

Then his phone rang. It was the Newark police. The driver of the taxi Mr. Quint was in—one Mohammed Khalil—had turned in the violin at the end of his shift. It was at the taxi stand right now. Did he want to come down and pick it up?

After he got the violin back, Mister Quint tracked down Mister Khalil. He thanked him, he embraced him, he pressed a $100 tip on him. Mister Khalil waved it all off. "Anyone would have done the same thing," he told a *New York Times* reporter.

Well, maybe for a cellphone or something . . . but a four-million-dollar violin??? "Everything we find is valuable to someone," said Mister Khalil. "If you lost your pen, you would think it was valuable."

Philippe Quint was feeling unfulfilled again. How could he show his gratitude?

Then it came to him—he would give a concert. Not at Carnegie Hall or the Lincoln Center, where Philippe Quint usually gave his concerts. At the Newark International Airport under a vinyl canopy in the parking lot by the taxicab holding area.

And he did. Quint played the theme from the movie *The Red Violin*. He played Gershwin's "It Ain't Necessarily So." He played a Paganini variation and the "Meditation" from Massenet's opera *Thais*.

The audience—some fifty cab drivers including Mohammed Khalil—loved it. They clapped and they danced. One of the drivers, a recent immigrant from Ghana, shimmied and moonwalked across the gravel to the music. "I like that he came here," the Ghanaian said, "And, yeah, the music, I like it."

So did the man responsible for reuniting Philippe Quint with Signor Stradivarius's creation. Mohammed Khalil sat front row centre, resplendent in his best black suit, with pink shirt and matching tie.

The day was a double celebration for Mohammed Khalil. Not only was he being honoured for his honesty, he was retiring. It was his last day of work.

Talk about going out on a high note.

HAVE A NICE %$#&ING DAY

All hockey players are bilingual. They speak English and profanity.

—GORDIE HOWE

ere's a fun experiment to try. Fill a big pail with ice water. Roll up your sleeve and dip your arm in up to your triceps. Say the first words that pop into your head. (Bad, right?) Now roll up your second sleeve and try the experiment with your other arm—only this time, when the shock of the cold threatens to shut down your heart, try substituting the word "handkerchief" or "Ronald McDonald" for the off-colour ones you used the first time.

Believe it or not, that is the gist of a scientific experiment recently carried out at Keele University in England. Richard Stephens was the psychologist behind the test. He got the idea from his wife, when she was in labour delivering their first child.

"Remember the breathing exercises, dear," he murmured helpfully to his beloved as she lay on the delivery table.

"Stick the @$%&*ing breathing exercises up your &%#, you inconsiderate mother<*&%#ing chauvinist pig @*@%$#&er," she growled.

Hmmm, thought Professor Stephens. I think I feel an experiment coming on.

He and his fellow researchers enlisted sixty-four volunteers. Rather than have them deliver babies, they were asked to submerge their arms in ice water for as long as they could. Half of them were encouraged to shout neutral words (like "eggplant" or "dining room table"; the other half got to shout out the choicest swear words they could think of.

The researchers were fairly certain that results would show that swearing had an adverse effect—in other words, uttering profanities would lessen the volunteers' resistance to pain. They figured the very act of swearing would subconsciously exaggerate the severity of the pain, thus lowering tolerance.

The researchers were dead wrong.

What the experiment showed was that swearing actually works. The volunteers who resorted to their favourite blue-tinged epithets could keep their arms submerged up to 40 percent longer than those who could only use emotionally uncharged words. The profanity-users also reported less pain and discomfort than the more polite participants.

Makes sense when you think about it. Swearing has probably been around since some nameless Neanderthal fumbled his sabre-toothed tiger haunch into the campfire and tried to fish it out with his bare hands. Swearing under stress is involuntary and it feels natural. Must be a good reason for it.

"It [swearing] has certainly been around for centuries," says Professor Stephens, "and is an almost universal human linguistic phenomenon." The professor and his colleagues theorize that swearing elevates the heart rate. A higher heart rate functions as a trigger to activate the primordial flight-or-fight response. Previous research has shown that this response temporarily lessens our sensitivity to pain, which in turn frees us to respond more quickly (and bravely) to external threats.

I have a feeling it doesn't hurt that a shouted mouthful of expletives also tends to make us look and sound tougher and more dangerous than we might actually be. As humorist Finley Peter Dunne observed, "Swearing was invented as a compromise between running away and fighting."

Whatever its origins, swearing has a long, if ignoble pedigree. Even as fine a writer as Mark Twain defended its usefulness.

"In certain trying circumstances, urgent circumstances, desperate circumstances," observed the author of *The Adventures of Tom Sawyer* and *Huckleberry Finn*, "profanity furnishes a relief denied even to prayer."

And Twain, for all his verbal facility, was an enthusiastic and frequent practitioner. The man swore—a lot. His wife Livy did everything she could to discourage Twain's use of profanity. One morning, after he'd cut himself shaving and delivered a long, loud and loquacious volley of curses, his wife confronted him, cleared her throat daintily and demurely repeated verbatim every X-rated syllable he had just uttered. Twain heard her out patiently, looked up to the ceiling, then shook his head sadly.

"You have the lyrics, my dear," he said, "but I'm afraid you'll never master the tune."

Damn! I wish I'd said that.

MENTIONING UNMENTIONABLES

Marge, you being the cop makes you the man . . . which
makes me the woman. I have no interest in that, besides
occasionally wearing your underwear, which, as we
discussed, is strictly a comfort thing.

—HOMER SIMPSON

Ah, yes . . . underwear. A.K.A. skivvies, BVDs, gotchies, draw-
ers, frillies, woollies, scanties, briefs, step-ins and unmention-
ables. Homer Simpson isn't the only soul whose knickers can tie him
up in knots. Consider the tragicomic plight of Joseph Espinoza and
Joaquin Rico.

Not exactly overachievers, Messrs. Espinoza and Rico. Their pri-
mary mission that Saturday evening was to hold up a Denver convenience store and avail themselves of whatever was in the cash register.
Being, as the phrase goes, "known to police," the duo wisely reasoned
that disguises might be in order. "Aha!" light-bulbed Joaquin. "How
about we put underwear over our heads?"

Not as stupid as it sounds, actually. Many a hold-up artist has
successfully distorted his facial features by wearing a nylon stocking
or even pantyhose over his head during the commission of his crime.
Alas, our banditos had neither, so they improvised.

They hit the store, intimidated the staff and got away with about
$100 cash and thirty-seven packs of cigarettes. But it wasn't long
before they were identified and arrested. Their disguises hadn't
been that successful. They'd robbed the store wearing underwear on

their heads, all right—Joaquin wore green; Joseph opted for blue. Unfortunately the desired masquerade effect was not forthcoming. The boys had chosen to wear . . . thong panties over their heads.

Poor Joaquin and Joseph—victims of their cultural times. If they'd been pulling heists in just about any other age, underwear disguises wouldn't have been an option. Cleopatra didn't wear panties. Cicero, pontificating splendidly in the Roman senate, had nothing on beneath his toga. Genghis Khan, marauding across the Asian steppes, rode bareback in the strictest sense of the word.

Humans didn't get serious about underthingies until the late nineteenth century, when a sadistic quack by the name of Dr. Gustav Jaeger came along advocating the health benefits of wearing coarse, undyed wool next to the skin. This was in Britain, naturally. Where else could the idea of wearing something hot and scratchy over your delicate bits be considered virtuous? For the next few decades, delusional Europeans and North Americans prided themselves on wearing undergarments that could hardly have been more uncomfortable.

And nowadays? Well, unlike Homer Simpson I can't speak knowledgeably about women's undergarments but as far as male attire goes, things aren't that bad. It pretty much comes down to a simple fashion choice of boxers or briefs. Wool, thank the gods, is out, and comfort is in. Underwear is as it should be—simple.

Which means of course that somebody had to figure out a way to make it complicated. That somebody seems to be Brazilian designer Lucia Lorio. She's marketing a feminine undergarment that contains a GPS chip enabling the wearer to be tracked by satellite. Why would anyone want such a thing? Why, for protection from terrorists and other assorted kidnappers. Feminist response has been decidedly cool. They want the device recognized for what they see it as: a virtual chastity belt allowing insecure males to keep track of their wives and/or sweethearts. Designer Lorio counters that the wearer has an on-off switch she can flip anytime she likes.

Which reminds me of the old chestnut about the English duke, off to fight in the Crusades, who made sure his Lady was securely encased in an iron chastity belt before he embarked. He locked the belt himself and secured the key on a gold chain around his neck. But the duke wasn't heartless. Realizing that he might end up dangling on the scimitar of a Saracen he entrusted a duplicate key to his loyal butler.

After his first day's journey the duke made camp at Dover in preparation for sailing to France in the morning. He was just about to turn in when he heard a galloping horse approaching. Moments later, his butler flung himself off the horse, red-faced and panting.

"My apologies, your Lordship," gasped the butler, "but you left the wrong key."

A LOAF OF BREAD,
A JUG OF WINE
AND A SINGING JACKKNIFE

*The lust for comfort. That stealthy thing that enters the
house as a guest, and then becomes a host, and then a
master.*

—KAHLIL GIBRAN

There was a Golden Age when the needs of humankind were
specific and few. Breathable air, clean water, a few turnips in the
larder and a woollen blanket on the bed. It wasn't enough, of course.
It never is for humankind. Enough for what? For everything, really.
Warmer blankets on the bed. Designer water by Evian and a Hardee's
Monster Thickburger with 1,420 calories and 107 grams of fat—more
than your average Somali family would see in a week.

Did you want fries with that?

We live in an age of wretched excess, folks. Did you ever think
you'd see a time when consumers would cheerfully lash out a couple
of hundred bucks for a pair of running shoes? Fifty dollars for a
short-back-and-sides from the barber? Four bucks for a Starbucks
coffee?

It gets worse. Herewith a six-pack of products on the market
you'd have to be nuts to crave, much less pay for.

Number one: the jigsaw puzzle alarm clock. This is a beauty
for all those masochists on your Christmas list. It's a timepiece

that doesn't merely jangle at 7 a.m.—it *explodes* like a Taliban IED (Improvised Explosive Device), spraying pieces of a jigsaw puzzle all over your bedroom. The kicker is—you have to assemble the jigsaw puzzle before the alarm will shut off! Isn't that *fun*? Crawling around half-awake among the dust bunnies under the bed in the pre-dawn gloom looking for shards of a jigsaw while the alarm howls like a banshee in the background? I can think of at least one giftee I'd love to send the jigsaw alarm clock to, but I'm not sure that in his current circumstances O.J. can accept gifts from the outside.

Number two: Poop Freeze. Sorry, this one's for pet owners only—and owners of incontinent pets at that. It's an aerosol freeze spray that, the manufacturers claim, forms "a frosty film on dog or cat poop to harden the surface for easy pickup."

Flash-frozen Rover scat! Whee! Be the first on your block, etc. (I kid you not. See www.poop-freeze.com.) Bring along your five-iron and you've got a whole new recreational diversion—the Poop 'n Putt Invitational.

Speaking of instruments of mass distraction, do you own a Swiss Army knife? You do? Well, trade it in because it's obsolete. I don't care if it's got the tweezers, the pincers, the magnifying glass, the fish scaler *and* the corkscrew with the eyeglass screwdriver attachment— it's Totally Yesterday.

What you need is the all-new Swissbeat. It's a knife with all the usual Swiss Army accoutrements—blade, nail file, scissors—plus an MP3 player, an FM radio and a voice recorder. Not to mention a remote control browser, high-quality earphones and a memory capable of storing up to 250 songs.

Not so much a jackknife as a home entertainment centre—on your belt. No charge for the hernia.

But hey, all this frenetic activity can wear a body down. You look like you're ready for a tall, cold one. How about a beer—a very special beer? You're in luck. Both Labatt and Molson have launched brand new brewskis that kick the slats out of traditional beers. We all know that beer makes you drowsy, fat and stupid, right? Not any more. This new beer from Labatt and Molson is chock-full of . . . *caffeine*. That's right—with the new beer, you can be *jumpy*, fat and stupid!

And if the beer doesn't give you a big enough buzz, shuck off your clothes, hop in the shower and lather yourself up with Shower

Shock. It's an all-vegetable-based glycerine bar soap that's been steeped in caffeine. The manufacturers claim that soaping up with Shower Shock will allow teensy-weensy molecules of caffeine to be absorbed by your skin. You may go into the shower as a dozy, somnolent sluggard, but a few minutes with Shower Shock and you'll tear back that shower curtain to face the world like a hyperventilating (albeit naked) ninja warrior.

Before your shower (and especially if you've had a Caffeinabeer or two) you might want to crayon the local EMO cardiac arrest unit phone number on your bathroom mirror, just as a precaution.

Ah, Brave New World. Where all a chap needs is a stereo pocket knife, an aerosol can of poop-freeze, one cold beer and a hot shower designed to make you nervous.

Excuse me. I'm going to check the larder for turnips.

PART FIVE

WAR? NO THANKS, I'D RATHER BE KNITTING

BOMB THEM WITH BLANKETS

So I get this email from a sender I don't recognize and it's head-lined "Books 'n Blankets." Against my better judgment, I open it and discover it's legit. It's from someone I do, in fact, know and she tells me her brother is a member of the Canadian military serving in Kabul. In his spare time over there he is personally handing out donated clothing, blankets and toys to needy Afghani kids. The details are heartbreaking. The email includes photos of a Canadian soldier doling out second-hand running shoes and used sweaters to solemn-eyed grade-school-aged kids who are barefoot or in plastic flipflops. This, in an Afghanistan winter.

"If anyone has gently used warm clothing items, blankets, shoes or toys to donate," the email says, "you can . . . drop them off at my place and I'd be happy to take care of the mailing."

What a splendid idea! We pack up a bunch of blankets, wool socks and sweaters that have been sitting at the back of our closet for years. We call the emailer up to see what time we can deliver the goods. "Please don't," she says. She has been totally overwhelmed at the response and can't possibly handle the volume.

Another goodwill gesture gone awry. It's not the first time that the best of intentions from outsiders have been frustrated in that baffling and beleaguered corner of the world. Back in 2004, some-body in the 1st Infantry Division of the US Army serving at a base about thirty kilometres north of Baghdad had a similarly splendid idea.

Iraqi kids, it seems, are soccer crazy. They love the sport and play pickup games in vacant lots, on empty streets—wherever they can. But they're poorer than dirt. Often they used wadded-up rags in place of a ball. Why not, some Yank wondered, as a goodwill PR gesture, hand out free soccer balls? The Army brass came onside, "Operation Soccer Ball" was born and eventually a five-ton truckload of soccer balls was ordered up and dispatched. Eager GIs lowered the tailgate, slashed open the first of dozens of cardboard boxes and found . . .

Soccer balls, yes—but deflated. And nobody had thought to include a pump or a needle valve to inflate them with. Army mechanics were baffled. They had the equipment to inflate the tires of Humvees and Jeeps, but not soccer balls. The sergeant in charge of Operation Soccer Ball radioed HQ and informed them of their dilemma. The order came down the line: "The Iraqis should be grateful. Hand 'em out anyway."

Orders are orders. The soldiers loaded the boxes into their vehicles and drove through towns and villages tossing out flaccid soccer balls to every kid they saw.

It was a PR disaster. "Kids were wearing them like hats," one soldier said. "They were in trees. They were floating in canals. They were everywhere."

What was supposed to be a goodwill gesture came off as a sneer, an insult. And the kids were pissed. "On our way back, kids were throwing rocks at us," the same soldier reported. "Maybe if we had given them inflated soccer balls, they would have been out playing soccer instead."

So it goes when one blunders into another culture of which one has little or no understanding.

Which got me thinking about that email I received. I wondered why this Canadian soldier—God bless him—is reduced to handing out second-hand clothing in his spare time over in Kabul? Why isn't the entire frickin' military handing out warm clothing—with a signature maple leaf logo on the label—full time?

Bound to be cheaper than bombs, tank rounds or ammo clips for AK-47s, right?

Canada is spending $100 million *a month* on military operations in Afghanistan. Experts reckon the price tag for Canadian taxpayers will have crested $7.2 billion by this spring.

We managed to put in some Tim Hortons outlets over there. We set up hockey rinks for our troops' rest and rec. Could we maybe slide some pullovers, tube socks and a Hudson's Bay blanket or two onto the tab?

Canada's hardest working folksinger, James Gordon, said it best in a song a few years ago:

Bomb them with butter, with rice and with bread
Bomb them with medicine and clothing instead.
Kill them with kindness, compassion and care.
Let them drink from clean waters, not the well of despair.
Get them right where they'll expect it the least
Bomb them with butter, attack them with peace.

Just a thought.

FEAR OF TERRORISM: THE NIPPLE EFFECT

For just a nanosecond it occurred to me that perhaps I'd died and gone to hell.

I was in a long line of cowed and daunted strangers, shuffling endlessly up stairs and down corridors under harsh fluorescent lights in an airless, dismally anonymous building toward an unknown destination. At the bottom of an escalator we were confronted by a portal, beside which stood a huge black man in a vaguely military uniform who was bellowing, seemingly at no one in particular:

"TAKE AFF YER BELTS, TAKE AFF YER SHOES, COINS, KEYS AND METAL OBJECTS OUTTA YER POCKETS AN INNA THE TRAY! TAKE AFF YER BELTS, TAKE AFF YER. . ."

He hollered his mega-decibel mantra over and over at the shambling wretches passing before him. Then I remembered that no, this wasn't hell. Just the seventh circle of airport security at LAX—Los Angeles International Airport, gateway to Asia–Pacific and institutional meat grinder to 61 million hapless passengers per year.

Welcome to Paranoiaville, post 9/11.

If you haven't had the experience of flying through LAX—or indeed, any major American airport in the past few years—my advice is simple: don't. Fly over the US, take a tramp steamer around it or better still stay home. You don't need the aggravation.

Can't fault their vigilance. I daresay that nary a tube of Colgate nor a set of toenail clippers have eluded the eagle gaze of Fortress America and its wand-waving minions. Woe betide the grey-haired granny who tries to board a flight with a pair of knitting needles tucked in her carry-on. Up against the wall, motherknitter!!!

Ever tried to commandeer a 747 with a pair of knitting needles? No. Neither has anyone else. Never mind.

Such sterling detection work doesn't come cheap. The world spends nearly US$6 billion a year patting down airline passengers in search of rocket launchers, Glock pistols and Improvised Explosive Devices. The good news is: last year, some 13 million prohibited items were intercepted and confiscated. The bad news? Most of them were Bic lighters.

Ever tried to commandeer a 747 with a Bic lighter? No. Neither has anyone else. Never mind.

And it's not as if they were all cigarette lighters. Some months back, Transportation Security agents on duty at the airport in Lubbock, Texas, were alerted by a metal detector that passenger Mandi Hamlin, en route to Dallas, had some undeclared metal on her person. They pulled her aside. An agent passed a hand-held wand in front of her chest.

Sure enough. The woman was trying to get on board wearing a pair of nipple rings. "They have to go," an agent said. Ms. Hamlin offered to show her breasts to a female agent—just to confirm she was wearing nipple rings, not hand grenades.

No dice.

They gave her a privacy curtain and a pair of pliers and insisted she remove them.

There can be, I understand, some pain involved in removing well-established nipple rings. With time, the flesh grows around them. Ms. Hamlin cried. She says she heard male agents snickering. Her attorney, Gloria Allred, is seeking—at the very least—an apology from airport security authorities. "Last time I checked," says attorney Allred, "a nipple was not a dangerous weapon."

Nevertheless, the madness continues—and spreads. In the near future, Vancouverites visiting their bank can expect a little extra attention—especially if they happen to be wearing a hat. Or sunglasses. "If they have ball caps on and sunglasses on, they'll be asked to remove the ball caps and sunglasses," says Sergeant Les Yeo of the Vancouver Police Board. Any exceptions? Pregnant moms? Decrepit old newspaper columnists? Kids on a peewee baseball team? Nope, says the sarge. "It'll be across the board."

Frankly, I find the Vancouver approach half-baked. I'd like to see RCMP identity checks and full body scans on people lining up to make their mortgage payments and check their deposits. In fact, why not have everybody do their banking in the nude?

Can't be too careful. Someone could be wearing a nipple ring.

WE HAVE MET THE ENEMY

Anybody out there old enough to remember Pogo? The swamp possum I mean, not the stick. As species go, Pogo is long past endangered and firmly on the extinct list, but back in the 1950s and '60s a cartoon strip of that name ran in over five hundred North American newspapers, delighting upwards of fifty million readers every week.

The strip (which was light years smarter than anything you'll find in most newspaper comic pages these days) was set in a mythical community in a swamp called Okefenokee. It featured a bizarre and memorable cast of talking animals including Pogo the possum—and also a paranoid mud turtle named Churchill (Churchy) LaFemme. Churchy saw nefarious government plots and Machiavellian political machinations in everything. The only reason I bring Churchy up—in fact, my entire purpose in writing these two paragraphs—is to inform you that I have a neighbour who looks unnervingly like Churchy LaFemme.

Thinks the same, too. The other morning as I walked the dogs past her place my neighbour yelled out to me, "When are you going to write about the chemtrails?"

"Chemtrails?" I riposted deftly.

She explained that chemtrails are the streaks in the sky left by secret government airplanes intent on spraying the earth with as-yet-unidentified substances. "Why would the government want to do that?" I asked. Churchy snorted. "Population control. Weather alteration. Superweapons biowarfare. Take your pick."

Ah, yes. *Those* chemtrails. It's a conspiracy theory that's been around for about a dozen years now—ever since some think tankers connected to the US Air Force drafted a strategic paper called "Owning the Weather in 2025." It was a blue-sky piece of abstract theory and the authors hastened to add it "did not reflect current military policy, practice or capability." Further, that "the US was not conducting any weather modification experiments and had no plans to do so."

Too late. The notion of governments purposely and secretly experimenting on their own populace found fertile ground in the primordial brainpans of Birthers, Truthers, Rapturists, Believers-in-Little-Green-Men-of-Roswell and others of the permanently paranoid persuasion. The Chemtrails Conspiracy Theory had achieved liftoff.

Evidence of any chemtrails project anywhere has since been denied by government officials around the world. In our own House of Commons the government house leader, Jay Hill, stood up and declared, "The term 'chemtrails' is a popularized expression and there is no scientific evidence to support their existence."

Pah. To a conspiracy theorist, a government denial is like spraying Quick Start on a brush fire. As Churchy would mutter, "What else would you expect them to say?"

At the risk of being outed as a government dupe and a lackey of the New World Order, I think what Churchy and his twitchy ilk are responding to are contrails, not chemtrails. Contrails have been with us since humans started hurling large metal objects high in the air. They consist of condensed water vapour coming off the wings and engines of airplanes and rockets moving through the atmosphere at high altitudes.

Chemtrailers say no, *con*trails disappear after a short while, whereas *chem*trails hang around and sometimes even turn into clouds. Air force experts say, on the contrary, some contrails do hang around for many hours, depending on atmospheric conditions. To chemtrail believers all I can say is, interesting theory. Too bad nobody with a shred of scientific credibility subscribes to it.

Contrails we definitely have—and the larger irony is that jet contrails really are hazardous to the health—ours and the planet's.

Contrails contain water, ice and soot, which together interfere with the dissipation of earth's energy. Tens of thousands of those stringy white lines form around the planet every day, knitting, in effect, a giant, ratty shawl that traps the earth's heat and contributes mightily to the greenhouse effect.

So—evidence that conspirators are seeding our skies with toxic chemicals in order to control the world and/or turn us all into zombies—or even worse—liberals? Pretty shaky. Chemtrails are a fantasy, but contrails are real and they really are messing up the atmosphere. And it's pretty hard to see that changing any time soon. Humans can perhaps be talked into recycling newspapers and sorting plastics, but giving up that cheap flight to Toronto or that Cancun weekend package? That's serious.

Pogo Possum said it best a half a century ago: "We have met the enemy," said Pogo, "and he is us."

GOOD NEWS IS NO NEWS

One Englishman is a story. Ten Frenchmen is a story.
One hundred Germans is a story. One thousand Indians
is a story. Nothing ever happens in Chile.

—NOTICE IN LONDON NEWSROOM

This is an embarrassing admission to make for someone who writes a newspaper column, but . . . I don't much follow the news anymore. Well, correction: I don't much follow the electronic news—i.e., radio, TV. I still dip my beak into the newspaper every day.

Why am I shunning news that comes over the airwaves? Because listening to or watching the news seems too much like sitting on a park bench next to some flaming methamphetamine addict who's obsessed with disaster and won't stop jabbering about it.

Newscasts on my radio and TV strafe me hour after hour and always on the hour with late-breaking news of earthquakes, tsunamis, fires, floods, insurrections and perturbations, most of them occurring at least five thousand miles from my doorstep. Yesterday, a news reader couldn't wait to tell me that an undisclosed number of unidentified citizens had perished in the crash of a passenger plane operated by a yet-to-be-verified national airline at the airport in Osh, Kyrgyzstan.

Here's a news flash for the news announcer: I'd be hard pressed to find Kyrgyzstan on the world map, never mind the bustling metropolis known as Osh.

Here's another news flash: I don't much care about what happens there.

I don't wish the paying customers of Air Anonymous ill. It's just that I can no longer embrace in their entirety the misfortunes of my planet. My arms won't stretch that wide. My compassion floppy disk is full.

Hell, even the local news is crammed with house fires, holdups and homicides involving strangers I don't know and will never meet. All of this might have greater relevance if I lived in New Jersey—or even along the Jane–Finch corridor. But I live, as do most Canadians, in a rather placid corner of a relatively Peaceable Kingdom. It's pretty quiet and unstrung where I live—at least until someone turns on the news.

I wonder, too, what profit there is in all the bad news that's foisted upon us? Not for the purveyors of bad news—that's obvious. There's an old saying in this business: If it bleeds, it leads. Conrad Black and Rupert Murdoch didn't make their bundles peddling tales of rescued kittens and happy Waltonesque homesteads.

But there's a societal blowback to the All Bad News All the Time phenomenon and Robert Hawkins exemplifies it. Hawkins? A forgettable loser. A druggie, a school failure and a punk so lame he couldn't even hold down a job at a McDonald's in Omaha. Why, we wouldn't know him at all if he hadn't put on that camouflage army uniform, picked up an AK-47, strolled into Westwood Mall in Omaha and blown away eight shoppers he'd never even seen before.

It wasn't his actions that made Robert Hawkins a household name. It was the fact that the media reported it. Hawkins may have been dim, but he knew how to grab a headline. In one of his last actions before he locked and loaded he scrawled a suicide note which concluded, "Just think tho, I'm gonna be ___ing famous."

Sure enough. He started firing and the camera crews and reporters were at the mall before the blood was dry. Robert Hawkins played those news pros like a pennywhistle. As one observer put it: "He knew he could count on his enablers: The media."

It didn't have to be. Your lives and mine were not enhanced by the sight of his face or the reporting of his name on the six o'clock news. Such details could have been withheld, just as reporters routinely withhold the names of rape victims or molested children.

Maybe such a voluntary action, opined columnist Mona Charen, "would tell nuts and loners they will no longer get the attention that they crave through an act of mass murder. Perhaps then we will deny oxygen to this terrible fire."

Maybe it would help snuff some other fires too. A couple of years ago intelligence authorities intercepted a letter from Ayman al-Zawahiri, Osama bin Laden's second-in-command, addressed to the leader of al-Qaeda in Iraq. "Don't forget," wrote Zawahiri, "that half of this battle is taking place in the battlefield of the media."

Put another way, the headlines generated by pipe bombs and suicide bombers are worth much more to terrorists than the paltry price of the lives expended. Back during the sixties, a seminal anti-war poster became briefly famous. It was drawn by a child and consisted of the words: "What if They Gave a War and Nobody Came?"

What would happen if a terrorist set off an IED and nobody reported it?

IT'S AN URBAN JUNGLE
OUT THERE

When a man is tired of London, he is tired of life; for there is in London all that life can afford.
—SAMUEL JOHNSON, 1777

Oh, I'm not so sure about that, Sam. I lived in London for a spell and it was rich and stimulating all right, but I'm not sure I'd dub it the absolute acme of civilization.

Granted, I lived there during the 1960s, not the 1770s. Johnson got to hobnob with Goldsmith, Swift and Fielding; the big names in my stint were Lennon, Harrison and McCartney. Johnson got to live and work in Grub Street. I got to shop for foppy shirts in Carnaby Street. Lively enough, to be sure, but somewhat exhausting and—dare I say it—ultimately a little tiresome.

If living in London taught me anything, it's that I'm not really suited to city life. That makes me—as usual—out of step with the times, because the human race has just passed a milestone. For the first time in the history of this planet, more people now live in cities than in the country. Imagine. We started out as nomads on the grasslands of Africa, evolving over centuries in our caves and huts and hovels. Over those centuries more and more of us migrated from the countryside toward that glow on the horizon. Now we've officially passed the urban-rural tipping point; most of us live in concrete jungles, bathed in bad air, continuous bedlam, twenty-four-hour artificial light, surrounded by millions of strangers.

Ain't progress wonderful?

There are lots of good reasons for city living of course. Operas, plays and the Cowboy Junkies don't tour much outside the city limits. Cities get the shopping malls and the swanky hotels and the five-star restaurants and you'll wait a long time to catch a live Leafs or Blue Jays game in the boondocks. But we pay a price for all that excitement. It makes us crazy.

Okay, that's overstating it, but only a little. A recent study by researchers at the University of Michigan confirms that just being in an urban environment impairs our mental processes. Hell, the study shows that *even a short walk* in the city takes its toll.

"The mind is a limited machine," says Marc Berman, who led the study. "And we're beginning to understand the different ways a city can exceed those limitations."

He has a point. Just think of what the human brain has to keep track of while taking a stroll down a city street. There's all those vehicles accelerating and braking, people whirring by on bikes and Rollerblades—all potentially dangerous. There are lampposts, telephone poles and buildings looming up and over our heads; curbs, trashcans and potholes at our feet. There's a blitzkrieg of noise—screeching tires, overheard radios, humming air conditioners, honking buses, kids yelling, the chatter of passersby on their cellphones. Plus we've got decisions to make. Should we check out that 20 percent off sale? Should we buy a copy of the *Walrus* or today's *Globe and Mail*? How about a soy cappuccino latte or a cold beer? Have I got a loonie for that homeless guy on the corner, and wow, check out the blonde in the Mercedes convertible.

And to process it all, we've got pretty much the same sized necktop wireless computer our forefathers had when they were wearing pelts and hunting for dinner with sharp sticks on the savannahs eons ago.

The poet Wilfred Owen once defined the typical North American city as a place that lacks everything from which no profit can be made. That's why in cities you can find lots of billboards but not too many trees; plenty of strip joints but precious few parks.

And that's a pity, because according to that University of Michigan study, serious green spaces are exactly what our cities need most. Results of the study show that our memory and ability to focus actually improve following time spent in nature, rather than in urban surroundings. The researchers say we need to look at green spaces not just as a pretty social amenity but as a form of therapy "with no known side effects, widely available and absolutely free."

Me? I spend at least an hour in deep therapy every morning of my life. I walk along a creek through firs and cedars. I often see deer, raccoons, ravens, chickadees, frogs and salamanders. Now and then there's a surprise appearance by a barred owl or a great blue heron.

I never see a Blue Jays double play or a Picasso exhibit or a Starbucks or a blonde in a Mercedes convertible, but that's okay—I still love my shrink.

She even lets me bring my dogs.

WATCH THE BORDERS

Back in the 1920s there was a debate in the Texas legislature over whether to introduce Spanish language instruction in state schools. Story goes that Miriam "Ma" Ferguson, the first female governor of Texas, ended the debate by standing up, waving a Bible and declaring, "If English was good enough for Jesus, it's good enough for the children of Texas."

Okay, the story is probably too good to be true, but it does resonate, especially for the several hundred million non-Americans around the world who get to watch the ongoing antics of the Excited States of America on a daily basis.

And most especially for Canadians. Try as they might (and they don't try very hard) most Americans suffer from North American tunnel vision. They simply cannot see their northern neighbours very clearly. Instead they take comfort in concocting Canadian myths. We all wear plaid. There's a Mountie on a horse outside every donut shop. We all say "aboot" and "hoose" for "about" and "house."

I have never heard a Canadian say aboot or hoose—have you?

Willie, the janitor on *The Simpsons*, maybe—but not a Canuck.

Americans tell themselves we "suffer" under socialized medicine in this country and that as a result, Canadians line up around the block to see a doctor and can't get into hospitals even for urgent surgery.

This from a country in which 47 million of its own citizens—18 percent of the population under sixty-five—have no medical insurance whatsoever.

When actor Natasha Richardson died following a fall while skiing in Quebec a few years back US tabloids blazed with cautionary headlines such as: "Socialized Medicine Killed Richardson." The fact that she was walking and talking after the fall and actually refused an ambulance wasn't mentioned by American reporters.

And then there's the terrorism thing. Shortly after the 9/11 attacks, several American TV commentators, radio show hosts and newspaper headline writers reported that the hijackers had infiltrated from Canada. Well, okay . . . it was a confusing time and rumours ran rampant. Turned out that not one of the hijackers—zero, zilch, ninguno—had entered the US from Canada. A spokesman for the Canadian government pointed that fact out in the House of Commons a few days after the attack. Peter Mansbridge mentioned it on *The National.* Frank McKenna, then-Canadian ambassador to the United States, called a press conference in Washington to correct the misapprehension.

But America wasn't listening.

In the ensuing nine years, Canada has been regularly and routinely bad-mouthed as a careless conduit for the 9/11 hijackers. Hillary Clinton told reporters the terrorists had crossed from Canada into New York. Texas congressman Ruben Hinojosa assured a congressional committee that the hijackers had crossed the border "using passports that Canadians accepted as valid despite the fact that the documents were doctored."

"It's something that won't go away," Bill Graham, Canada's defense minister, moaned back in 2003. "We're very resentful . . . because not one suspect had been in Canada. All had been in the US, training in the US, with valid US visas."

That's right, America. It was *your* border guards, not ours, that waved the hijackers through customs. You even went so far as to teach them how to pilot passenger jets.

But it's a correction that American ears won't hear. As recently as 2009 Janet Napolitano assured reporters that the 9/11 hijackers had come through Canada. Later she said that she'd been misunderstood, but she's on tape, and the tape doesn't lie.

She's *the head of US Homeland Security*, for cripes' sake.

And just days after that John McCain—who could have become the president—repeated the bogus legend yet again.

Ah, well. When it comes to borders Americans have always tended toward the paranoid and illogical. There is the story of FBI director J. Edgar Hoover and his penchant for scribbling his views in bright blue ink in the margins of memos and reports he received from underlings. Sometimes he would fill all four borders of a typewritten sheet with his observations handwritten with a fountain pen. Once an assistant made the mistake of sending him a typewritten page in which the copy ran almost to the edges of the paper, leaving Hoover very little room to write.

"WATCH THE BORDERS!" Hoover printed in angry, bright blue block letters across the top of the page.

And nothing moved across the Canadian and Mexican frontiers for the next five days.

YARNBOMBERS? SHOE NUFF

Men love war because it allows them to look serious.
Because it is the only thing that stops women laughing
at them.

—JOHN FOWLES

I'm not big on war heroes, but if I had to pick one, I'd choose Muntazer al-Zaidi.

Never heard of him? Sure you have. He's the Iraqi journalist who threw his shoes at then-US president George W. Bush in Baghdad.

Gotta love the optics—smirky, smug and swaggering leader of the most bellicose and heavily armed nation on the planet cringing under the onslaught of a pair of incoming wingtips. The shoes missed their mark and that's a good thing, too. No physical damage done, but the most powerful anti-war statement since a kid in a white shirt faced down a column of Chinese army tanks in Tiananmen Square.

Who knows? After years of murder and mayhem in Iraq and Afghanistan, Palestine and Israel, Sudan and Zimbabwe, perhaps the quaint concept of non-violent protest is making a teensy-weensy comeback. That would explain the Yarnbombers.

Never heard of them either? You will. Their strike capacity is international in scope. Yarnbombers have already left their mark on the Great Wall of China, France's Notre Dame cathedral and San Francisco's Golden Gate bridge. In Mexico City they immobilized a city bus.

And if you think the placid Great White North is immune from attack, think again. Yarnbombers have already struck in Vancouver and Montreal. Chances are you'll see their handiwork around your hometown someday very soon.

Yarnbombing, or Stealth Knitting as it's also known, started, ironically enough, in Bush's home state of Texas a few years ago. A bunch of frustrated knitters sitting around in Houston got to talking about half-finished sweaters, abandoned doilies, dust-gathering balls of yarn *and* the woefully shabby and soulless appearance of their downtown area . . . and suddenly the light went on.

What if a guerrilla team of craftspeople, operating in secret and under cover of darkness, just went out and adorned the uglier parts of the neighbourhood with . . . knitting?

Thus was born Knitta, the world's first gang of derring-do darners and crochet commandos. Their mandate is simple: cloak everything from bar stools to utility poles with vibrant, colourful hand-stitched works of art.

As I said, the movement has since gone global. In Paris in 2007, thousands of pairs of knitted socks suddenly appeared on street corners and café tables in the Marais district. In Mexico City a team of commandos knitted up a mammoth tea cosy that covers an entire bus (which has since been retired and turned into an arts studio). Here in Canada, yarnbombers first surfaced in Quebec last year, where, one January morning, Montrealers awoke to find several *Arret* signs sporting snug and nifty knitted tubes around their poles. In Vancouver's Strathcona district a local yarnbomber—or perhaps a brigade of them—has been knitting mantillas for wire fences, leg warmers for utility poles and pompoms for car antennae.

Yarnbombing isn't anti-war per se. In fact it isn't *anything* per se. It's just . . . freelance knitting. Yarnbombers frequently take flak for what's perceived as a lack of practicality. Why aren't they knitting sweaters and socks for widows and orphans? Afghans for Afghanis and turtlenecks for abandoned seals? Why don't they do something *useful*, for crying out loud? What's the point of knitting woollen graffiti for park benches, lawn ornaments and stop signs?

There is no point.

That's the point.

Mandy Moore, a Vancouver practitioner, told a *Globe and Mail* reporter that she and her colleagues reject the hoary tradition of knitting products for altruistic causes.

Yarnbombers do it just for the hell of it.

And why not? There's something life-affirming and whimsical about "found" knitting that serves no useful purpose other than to make an object look less industrial, more cared for. Best of all, it does no harm. Guerrilla knitting doesn't damage property. And if it's your property and you disagree the remedy is simple: tear it off. But it makes you look like Mr. Crankypants.

The comedian Elaine Boosler once riffed on the deceptively pacific names we assign to "anti-personnel devices"—a.k.a. weapons of terror and death.

"Peacekeeper missile," she mused. "Doesn't that sound like axe-murderer babysitter?"

Indeed. Give me yarnbombers and shoe tossers anytime.

AS A MARTYR OF FACT . . .

*When fascism comes to America it will be wrapped in a
flag and carrying a cross.*

—Sinclair Lewis

I read the news today, oh boy . . .

—The Beatles

A guy could get awfully depressed reading the news these days.
Joe Wilson, a peanut-brained Republican congressman from
South Carolina, gratuitously and publicly insults the president.
Historically, this is not a career-enhancing move. Squeaky Fromme
tried it on President Ford in 1975 and spent the next thirty-four years
in the slammer. When Iraqi Muntazer al-Zaidi hurled a Hush Puppy
at George Bush he went to jail too. He surfaced some months later
with two broken ribs and a smashed foot.

Joe Wilson? Dissing Obama made him a folk hero to the
Republican lunatic fringe. Donations to his campaign office went up
by a million bucks in the next week alone.

Oh, and he was praised as a valiant patriot from the pulpit of his
church the following Sunday.

We live in crazy times with crazies at home and crazies abroad.
But a lot of them have one thing in common: they are very religious.
Fanatically so.

Zealots on the other side of the water cable-stitch explosives into
their suicide cardigans and dream of being serviced in the afterlife by
seventy-two virgins. Is that so much stranger than the zealots on this

side who think Obama is the Antichrist and seriously contemplate the coming of the Rapture?

The Rapture—that Disneyesque day a-comin' when the Goodly among us will spontaneously shed their clothes, their credit cards and their car keys and levitate magically upward through the elms to live for eternity above the clouds, leaving the rest of us unsaved and ungodly sods to duke it out here in Hell On Earth. You want to really get depressed? Some polls say as many as 55 percent of Americans buy into the notion of the Rapture.

Stephen King couldn't make this stuff up.

We live in an age when access to information has never been freer and the ocean of knowledge has never been deeper, yet as near as I can tell way too many of us are stupider than ever. I can only see three responses to this pathetic speed bump in human development: get mad, get sad or laugh our butts off.

Some people are embracing Option Three. A new website is extending a helping hand to all pet-owning Rapture believers by offering a post-Rapture pet care service. Simply put, for a mere $110 per critter, the folks at Eternal Earth-Bound Pets will look after all the dogs, cats and cockatoos that sky-bound Rapturites will be leaving behind.

Naturally, there's some fine print. If the subscribers lose their faith or are not "Raptured" within the next ten years, they are not entitled to a refund.

Eternal Earth-Bound Pets employees are all atheists, but as their website points out, that turns out to be a Good Thing. They're definitely going to be left behind and thus can be counted on as reliable kibble and cat chow dispensers.

Facetious? Maybe, but there's nothing tongue-in-cheek about the email service being offered by Mark Heard. Subscribers to his service, called Youvebeenleftbehind, get to send up to sixty-three post-Rapture emails after the sender has been whisked off the Earth and transported to Heaven. The inspiration came to Heard, a Christian, after it occurred to him that he would not be able to send his wife important passwords if the Rapture should suddenly sweep him, but not her, skyward. "This gives you," says Heard, "one last chance to reach your lost family and friends for Christ."

Meanwhile, on the other side of the divine divide, television station Kanal T in Istanbul is about to air a reality show variation. In this version, ten atheists will try to resist conversion by a priest, a rabbi, a Muslim imam and a Buddhist monk. The winner, if any, gets an all-expenses paid trip to the Holy Land (Vatican, Jerusalem, Mecca, Tibet) of whichever faith he or she converts to.

Stephen King couldn't make this up either.

Still not laughing? Then let me leave you with Robin Williams' take on the al-Qaeda belief that seventy-two virgins wait to entertain "martyrs" when they get to the other side.

"My only hope," says Williams, "is that when those terrorists get to heaven, they meet up with the kind of virgins we had in Catholic school: Sister Mike Ditka from Our Mother of Eternal Retribution."

THE SKY IS FALLING! MAYBE

Creative visualization time, kiddos. I want you to imagine a rock. I'm not talking gravel here, or even boulders. The rock we're conjuring up is as wide as three football fields. It's black, it's gnarly and it's hurtling through space just as fast as a big space rock can hurtle.

Let's give it a name. Let's call it—oh, I don't know—Apophis! Yeah, Apophis.

Oh, look—Apophis is getting bigger! It's getting bigger all the time!

Actually, that's an optical illusion. Apophis isn't really swelling, it just seems like that because, because . . .

It's heading right toward us.

This is not a fantasy exercise. There really is an asteroid named Apophis and it really is headed our way. Should arrive in twenty-seven years, give or take a week. The good news is, it won't hit us.

Probably.

A few years back, scientists weren't so sure. Back in 2004, astronomers were getting just the teensiest bit agitated about the space asteroid they'd identified and dubbed Apophis after an ancient Egyptian serpent god. Believe it or not, the name was an improvement. Earlier they'd dubbed the asteroid 2004 MN4. They calculated its trajectory and decided there was a chance that the asteroid could be entering earth's atmosphere about 2029. Later they decided that 2036 was the more likely date.

Such an occurrence is far from rare. Fact is, the earth is constantly bombarded by a veritable blitzkrieg of space rocks—about 200,000 a day. Most of them, however, are either microscopic or at least have the decency to incinerate themselves when they hit the oxygen of our atmospheric envelope. About 150 morsels of space detritus actually survive long enough to hit our planet's surface, but they're mostly tiny and hardly ever even noticed.

How much damage would an asteroid as wide as three football fields cause, ploughing into the earth? Depends on where the ploughing gets done. If Apophis came down in the middle of the boreal forest or far out in the Pacific or the Atlantic the result would be merely an ecological catastrophe. If it barrelled into us at, say, the intersection of Yonge and Bloor it would constitute one of the worst disasters in recorded history (and give the Leafs their best excuse yet for a dismal season).

Mind you, it wouldn't be as cataclysmic as the meteorite that hammered northern Quebec a few millennia ago. Scientists don't know exactly how big that one was, but it was a monster. And it left a seven-and-a-half-mile-wide divot now famously known as the Pingualuit Crater. And then there's the one that many scientists believe caused the extinction of the dinosaurs. The theory is that a massive prehistoric meteor strike around the Yucatan peninsula area ushered in a "nuclear winter" that destroyed much of the life on our planet.

But strikes of that magnitude are blessedly rare. In fact, scientists have calculated that a meteor strike causing a thousand human deaths or more "is unlikely" to occur once in a million years.

Which is somewhat comforting—until you realize there's no reason that one couldn't cream us next Thursday.

As for Apophis, you can come up out of the root cellar. Scientists are now saying that particular galactic cannonball probably won't come within 18,000 miles of planet Earth.

But . . .

Apophis still has them worried. Problem is, 18,000 miles still amounts to a close brush in space terms and nobody knows just how that close encounter with earth's gravitational field will affect the orbit of Apophis. Steve Chesley, an astronomer who works with the Near-Earth Object lab in Flintridge, California, says, "The deflection caused by the 2029 encounter will be significant. We're worried about its future trajectory. The next time Apophis is expected to be in our neighbourhood is in the year 2068." Chesley reckons there's a one-in-three-hundred-thousand chance of Apophis hitting the earth on that date.

I'm cool with that. In 2068 I'll be turning 125. Even if by some miracle I'm still alive I'll be too far gone to know my asteroids from a hole in the ground.

WARNING: ILLEGAL FURNITURE

The bench appeared right in the middle of town, overnight and seemingly out of nowhere. You knew right away that it wasn't a government-approved project because . . . well, for one thing it *did* appear overnight. If taxpayers had been footing the bill there would have been a week of flyers, a gauntlet of wooden barricades, a posted, plasticized work permit and a maintenance crew of at least six guys in fluorescent overalls filing time cards for a minimum of two eight-hour shifts.

But no. What we had was an empty space at sundown, filled with a brand new bench the next morning.

The other dead giveaway was the fact that the bench was clearly not standard municipal issue. The thing was hand-hewn, unpainted and definitely on the funky side.

One other distinctive feature: it had what appeared to be the anchor chain from a good-sized yacht securing it to a nearby lamppost.

This bench wasn't going anywhere anytime soon.

Explanation? This addition of outlaw urban furniture was my town's introduction to a movement that is sweeping the world in its own quiet way. It is called "guerrilla benching"—the unauthorized installation, by persons unknown, of a bench or other item into a public space. Apparently some public-spirited citizens decided our town needed a bench, didn't want to wait around for the wheels of bureaucracy to grind one out, so they just went ahead and installed it.

And the anchor chain? That was to discourage municipal bureaucrats from "uninstalling" the impromptu bench.

Nobody seems to know who's responsible, just as no one seems to know exactly where guerrilla benching got its start. It might have been in London, England, where a whole flotilla of wooden benches appeared on sidewalks after Camden Council began removing park benches that had been there for years.

In New York, guerrilla knitters have taken up a cozy variation of the challenge. They've wrapped telephone poles and traffic standards in bright and saucy creations that look a lot like leg warmers.

The French have been even more ambitious. Last year a team of underground (literally) activists infiltrated the Pantheon, the venerable mausoleum in downtown Paris where France's most illustrious expired citizens are entombed. There, after hours and under cover of darkness over a period of several weeks, they . . . repaired a 150-year-old clock that was rusting away from official neglect.

When the clock, which hadn't worked for decades, suddenly began chiming the hours, French bureaucrats (choose one):

(a) Wept with joy and conferred the *Légion d'honneur* on the guerrillas;

(b) Donned ceremonial uniforms of sackcloth and ashes and fired themselves for negligence and incompetence;

(c) Sued the clock repairers for break and entry, threatening them with huge fines and jail time.

You guessed it. As one of the Pantheon infiltrators puts it: "We could go down in history as the first people to go to jail for repairing a clock."

The Pantheon guerrillas are one more example of a fascinating development in urban behaviour—the reclaiming of public spaces on behalf of the, er, public. We all know what you get when bureaucrats are left in charge of public spaces. You get University Avenue in Toronto—a die-straight surgical slash through the belly of the city as sterile and deserted as a shopping mall after hours.

But something vibrant happens when actual, unpaid human beings get involved. Some people call it placemaking—an attempt by local communities to look at their streets, parks, buildings and markets with the idea of making them people-friendly.

And it doesn't have to involve breaking the law. Portland, Oregon, has a posse known as the City Repair Project, an all-volunteer group that gets locals involved in fixing up their own communities with everything from a clean sweep to a new paint job.

On a suburban street in Victoria, BC, there's a wacky-looking, brightly painted cupboard that stands by the curb. It has a glass door that just barely contains the contents—dozens and dozens of slightly used hardcovers and paperbacks.

This is the Clare Street Book Exchange box. People in the neighbourhood pick up or drop off books—and incidentally get to chat with other neighbours who are doing the same thing. Who put the box there? Search me. What are they trying to prove? Who cares? It works. And it makes for a friendlier, more cohesive neighbourhood.

And there's not a damn thing the bureaucrats can do about it.

DE=SCOTTISHIFY? OCH!

That garret of the earth—that knuckle-bone of
England—that land of Calvin, oat-cakes and sulphur.

That would be Sydney Smith running off at the mouth. Smith
was an English clergyman, essayist and wit, a contemporary of
Napoleon and Beethoven and, obviously, no great friend of Dear
Auld Scotland, which is what he was slagging for being an attic, a
skeletal leftover and a repository of brimstone religion and bad food.
Mister Smith must have been possessed of an admirable set of gonads
to bad-mouth Scotland that way, considering that he was ordained
as a minister in Edinburgh and even helped to found the esteemed
Edinburgh Review in 1802.

He's not the only famous name to take a flinty view of Scotland.
Lord Byron called it "a land of meanness, sophistry and lust." Charles
Lamb sniffed, "I have been trying all my life to like Scotchmen, and
am obliged to desist from the experiment in despair." That curmudgeon's curmudgeon, Samuel Johnson, grumbled, "The noblest
prospect which a Scotchman ever sees is the high road that leads him
to England."

Harsh words, laddies—although to be fair, Scotland does have
a few things to answer for. Argyle socks hop to mind. Closely followed by haggis, plaid shirts, kilts, porridge and caber tossing—all
accompanied, of course, by the banshee keening of a set of Highland
bagpipes.

I haven't even mentioned Scotland's most cursed bequest to the world. (Hint: it involves dressing up in geeky clothes in order to take long walks in faux-wilderness surroundings punctuated by acts of personal flagellation and self-mortification inflicted with a variety of clubs and cudgels specifically designed for the aforementioned exercise in embarrassment.)

Ah, yes. No accident that, backwards, it spells "flog."

On the other hand, Scotland also bequeathed us Robbie Burns and single-malt scotch. Not a bad bargain.

And oh, yes—Canada as we know it.

If the Great White North could show the ribbons and strains of Scottish blood absorbed just in the exploration of this land—the Mackenzies and Frasers, the Thompsons and Raes, the Douglases and Dunsmuirs—we'd have a brand new tartan on our hands.

Those early Scots–Canadians mastered parchment as well as paddles. The names of the first six prime ministers of Canada carry a certain burr: Macdonald, Mackenzie, Macdonald, Abbot, Thompson, Mackenzie Bowell.

For a mere knucklebone of England, Scotland has made a rather impressive international splash over the centuries. It's interesting, then, that there's a move afoot to stamp all that out. And more interesting still that the initiative for the move comes from Scotland itself.

It's even given the English language a brand new word: de-Scottishification.

This profoundly ugly mouthful means "to rebrand a product or a company in order to play down or remove its Scottish connotations."

Why would any company want to divorce itself from its Scottish background? It all has to do with the decision this year by the Scottish government to release Abdelbaset al-Megrahi, a.k.a. the Lockerbie Bomber. The man had been found guilty of involvement in the aircraft bombing that took 270 lives over Scotland. In 2001 he was sentenced to life imprisonment, but the Scottish government cut him loose and sent him back to Libya—a decision thought to be not unconnected to a massively favourable oil deal between Scotland and that country.

Whatever the politics, it was a PR disaster for Scotland, leading to worldwide calls for a boycott of all Scottish businesses. The Hebrides company that manufactures the famous Harris tweed fabric blinked. The company has dropped the word "Scottish" from all of its North

American marketing campaigns. "We have been getting a lot of [negative] feedback and we have had to 'de-Scottishify' the image of the brand," said a company spokesman.

No more Harris tweeds? What next—a blackout of all Sean Connery movies? Do we have to rename Scotch broth, Scotch tape and Scotch eggs?

At the risk of compounding its misery, I think Harris tweed should be cited for contempt.

Of the English language. "De-Scottishification"? Ugh. Even Sydney Smith wouldn't stoop that low.

PART SIX

WEIRD SCIENCE

TEN-FOUR CB, MAY YOU RIP

Last Saturday morning I found myself halfway up the side of a mountain—not Himalayan-scale, but creditable. I wasn't swinging across crevasses or sucking on oxygen cylinders but I was up there, all right. High enough to be looking down at the backs of bald eagles soaring below me; high enough to watch popcorn balls of cloud scudding through a stand of fir at eye level across a valley.

I was well beyond the urban grid and the telephone wires, up there on my high lonesome, a couple of hours' walk from my fellow man and all of his works.

So I did what any intrepid, pioneering explorer type deep in the wilderness—Thor Heyerdahl, Sir Edmund Hillary, Dr. David Livingstone—would have done in my situation.

I whipped out my cellphone, called up my local bookstore and reserved a Saturday copy of the *Globe and Mail.*

Cheap thrill? Sure, I guess. But I'm an old guy—so old I actually remember the great grandfather of that slim little lozenge I was holding to my ear up that mountain.

Anybody else out there remember citizens' band radio?

Seems ludicrous now, but thirty years ago the modern cellphone was as unreachable and futuristic as Mister Spock's phaser. What we had instead were black and shiny hand-held microphones attached by curlicue cords to the underside of our dashboards. It was called

CB (for citizens' band) radio and yes, you did require that one extra component in order to be a dyed-in-the-ether CBer.

You needed an automobile. Or, ideally, an articulated ten-ton semi. CBs began life as the preferred means of communication for North American long-haul truck drivers. Those guys used their CBs to keep in touch with fellow truckers on the job. In the early stages of its evolution, CB radio was actually useful. Truckers could warn fellow knights of the road about blizzards, washouts, rock slides and traffic jams up ahead.

Not to mention government inspectors, radar traps and cute waitresses.

CB wasn't just a communications device, it was a cultural phenomenon. A CB "slanguage" sprang up. Cops weren't cops; they were "smokeys" or "bears" (a "smokey on four legs" was a Mountie). Instead of "Hello" a CBer said "Come on," with an interrogative lilt at the end. As in: "Toledo Ted, this here's Ruptured Rabbit, come on?"

That was the other thing about the CB culture. You couldn't just be Fred or Tony. You had to give yourself a "handle" like Winnipeg Willie or Saskatoon Slim.

CB even inspired a Top Ten song—"Convoy"—a mawkish, talkin'-country saga about a bunch of rebellious truckers fed up with paying exorbitant highway tolls. Sample lyric:

I could see the bridge was lined with bears but I didn't have a dog-gone dime.

I sez Pig Pen, this here's the Rubber Duck, we just ain't a-gonna pay no toll.

Oh, yeah—and to be really authentic, you had to make yourself sound like a Tennessee hillbilly—lots of "this heres" and "a-gonnas."

Sounds ridiculously hokey and maybe it was, but CB seemed to work just fine when it was solely the purview of the burly, flat-bummed jockeys of tanker trucks and big cargo rigs. It sounded painfully dumb when high school kids in their dad's station wagons or accountants in Audis tried it on.

There were technical problems too. Solar flares, for some reason, played hell with CB reception, as did the sheer onslaught of millions of fad-chasing amateurs who clambered aboard the CB bandwagon in the late '70s and early '80s. Reception was unpredictable and haphazard under normal conditions. Hordes of day trippers swamping the airwaves just made it worse. In the end CB proved to be the technological equivalent of a dinosaur with glass ankles. It collapsed from its own weight.

Just as well. I'm a certified technophobe but when I compare those old, clunky CB units and the phoney, mock-jock good old boy personas that went with them to the modern mobile phone, a wire-free gizmo smaller than a deck of cards that can take pictures, send emails, download *Seinfeld* episodes *and* allow me to talk with crystal clarity to my cousin in Mississauga or an old school buddy in Melbourne, Australia, even I have to admit that some technological advances are—to quote my Melbourne buddy—bloody marvellous, mate.

And that's a ten-four, good buddy.

TAKE THAT PHONE
AND SHOVE IT

I t's official: the alarm clock is no longer the most hated technological device on the planet. A study by researchers at the Massachusetts Institute of Technology has conferred that dubious honour on (flourish of beeps, squawks and the opening bars of Beethoven's Fifth) . . . the cellphone.

Or "yell phone," as I like to think of it. Why is it that people who insist on yapping on their cells in public think they have to holler like a lumberjack to be heard? It might be different if the conversations (the one side of it we get to hear, at least) were entertaining, but they never are. They're about late invoices, dental appointments, school pickups or breathless, late-breaking "travel updates."

"YEAH, FRANK . . . BILL HERE. I'M IN TERMINAL TWO RIGHT NOW. JUST GOT OFF THE CALGARY FLIGHT. MY FLIGHT TO MONTREAL DOESN'T LEAVE FOR FORTY MINUTES SO I SHOULD BE DOWNTOWN BY . . ."

Too much information, buddy.

What a phenomenon, the cellphone. I remember visiting Italy a few years back and being dumbfounded by all the mentally incapacitated natives walking down the street holding their ears and talking to themselves. "They're talking on cellphones, dummy," my partner explained.

Oh, yeah. Right. I knew that.

Italy—in fact, much of Europe—had long been famous for its wretched telephone service, so it wasn't surprising that when cellphone technology arrived, it was gobbled up like an all-dressed pizza. Here in Canada we had a pretty decent telephone system in place, so cellphones took a little longer to establish a beachhead.

Well, they've landed. At last report 13.5 million Canadians subscribe to a cellphone service and the numbers are still soaring skyward.

Too bad cellphone etiquette hasn't kept up. I used to take a perfectly wonderful early morning ferry ride that was ruined by a single cellphoniac. Ferry passengers—regulars mostly—used to convene at tables in a large common cabin where we sipped our coffee, read the paper or kibitzed in a low-key, early morning kind of way.

Then the jerk with the cellphone arrived. A building contractor. He commandeered one of the tables, hauled out his cellphone and commenced to call a long list of customers and suppliers, barking out job quotes, service orders, work crew instructions and other assorted business crap that only two people in the universe could possibly have been interested in. The rest of us melted into the corners but you couldn't get away from the guy. He had a voice like Don Cherry. I complained to one of the crew who shrugged apologetically. "There's no law against it," he said. He was right. Unfortunately.

The cellphone has not only shattered our privacy it has imbedded itself in our language. We have the "cell yell" (already ranted upon); we also have the hammy offshoot known as "stage phoning," wherein some Suit flamboyantly flourishes his Fido at a restaurant table and proceeds, with much windmilling of arms and mock opera gestures, to impress the clientele with just what a Big Time Operator he is.

Then there's the highway and byway phenomenon known as DWY—Driving While Yakking. I haven't seen the accident statistics for people who have ploughed into trees or been T-boned by a semi while chatting on their mobiles, but I'll bet they're impressive.

Other signs that cellphones are here to stay? The resistance that's building up to them. One of Japan's hottest exports this year is a product called "Magnetic Wood." It's a kind of building material panelling that's saturated with magnetic particles of nickel-zinc ferrite. This apparently deflects 97 percent of mobile-phone signals.

More and more restaurant owners and barkeeps are lining their walls with the stuff so that their clientele can eat and drink in relative peace and quiet. I also note that July has been declared "Cellphone Courtesy Month" and that Amtrak—the Yankee equivalent of VIA Rail—has begun to introduce "Quiet Cars" on its commuter runs, wherein the mobile phone is banned.

Other jurisdictions have a long way to go. Down in the Sunshine State, the California Highway Patrol estimates that 40 percent of the emergency 911 calls they receive each year are false alarms caused by people accidentally parking their behinds on their cellphones.

"Butt Calls," the cops call them.

I call it Appropriate Stowage.

NO DUMPING ALLOWED

So I'm sitting in this meeting one afternoon last week and it's not too bad, as meetings go. I've got a comfortable chair, the speaker's not putting me to sleep and best of all I've got a cup of good, hot coffee steaming in my favourite double-walled stainless steel travel mug. It's sitting on the table in front of me.

That's when the guy next to me leans over and whispers, "Is that your coffee cup?"

"Yeah, it is," I whisper back.

"Because," he whispers, "I left my coffee cup at a meeting here last week."

"That's my cup," I whisper back.

"My coffee cup looked exactly like that," he whispered.

"That's my cup," I assure him, in a louder, more assertive whisper.

"You're sure?" he whispers, doubtfully.

"NO, YOU CRETIN! THAT'S YOUR CUP! I SNUCK IN HERE OVER THE WEEKEND, STOLE YOUR CUP AND BROUGHT IT IN TO FLAUNT IT IN FRONT OF YOUR FACE THIS AFTERNOON TO SEE IF YOU'D NOTICE!"

I didn't say any of that of course, but that's what was running through my mind—that, along with several Howard Stern-worthy adjectives that would be unseemly to repeat.

Thing is, I spent the rest of the day in a smouldering funk. I cold-shouldered the receptionist, snapped at a couple of my colleagues—even yelled at my computer. The guy absolutely ruined my afternoon. The rest of my working day was a total write-off.

And all over a coffee cup.

I probably would have had a lousy evening too, except for something that happened on the way home. A neighbour gave me a lift, and as we were driving through town, a lout in a Trans Am came squealing out of a side street, went into a four-wheel drift and came within a hair of side-swiping us. My neighbour honked to warn him off.

Incredibly, the Trans Am goon leans out his window and lets fly with a string of curses at my neighbour, punctuated with an exclamation mark graphically illustrated by an upraised digit on his left hand.

I am unhinged. I am furious. I want my neighbour to stop the car so I can go over to this clown and . . .

But I glance at my neighbour and see that he is . . . *smiling* at the idiot in the Trans Am. Giving him a cheery wave and a big Have-a-Nice-Day smile.

"What was *that*?" I ask my neighbour. "That guy could have killed us! He was totally in the wrong!"

My neighbour shrugged, still smiling. "He was probably having a bad day," he said. "No point in us getting bummed out too."

My neighbour went on to explain that he had this theory. He figured a lot of people went through life imitating sanitation trucks. They picked up all this trash all day long—petty frustrations, little snubs and insults—and pretty soon they were overloaded. They had to find someone else to dump it off on.

"The thing I try to remember is, when somebody gets in my face, it's not about me," he said. "It's nothing personal. That person is just trying to unload his trash and I happen to be there. If I let them tick me off, then bingo! I've let them dump on me. But I don't have to accept their trash. I can just smile, wish them well and wave goodbye."

And I thought: Wow. All the fights that I've been in; all the arguments and shouting matches; the scuffles and the hissy fits; all the bluster and the bullshit . . .

All because I imagined that someone had insulted me, tweaked my pride. What a waste of time. What a waste of energy.

In "Restless Farewell," Bob Dylan sings:

Oh every foe that ever I faced
The cause was there before we came.

I first heard those lyrics in the sixties. Took me half a century to "get" them.

I figure I've just learned a lesson and I'm going to try and put it to good use, but first I've got one last score to settle.

I'm going to track down that guy who bugged me at that meeting last week.

I want to ask him if he'd like my coffee cup.

PAPER OR PLASTIC?
WILD OR FARMED?

Anyone who isn't confused doesn't really understand the situation.

—EDWARD R. MURROW

I admit it—I'm deeply confused. Every day I am offered simple, no-nonsense, unambiguous advice from Greenpeace, David Suzuki, the Sierra Club, Al Gore, Oprah and the grade six class of Salt Spring Elementary School as to exactly What I Ought to Be Doing to Save This Planet . . .

And every day I just get more and more confused.

It begins at the supermarket checkout counter. "Will that be paper or plastic?" the clerk asks me. And I think to myself, well, let me see. Would I prefer to decimate what's left of Canada's old-growth forests by having my groceries bundled into paper bags, or . . . Should I continue to contribute to the West's slavish dependence on foreign oil by using petroleum-derived plastic bags—which, being non-biodegradable, will of course go on to moulder sullenly in some landfill site for untold millennia?

(And for those environannies who are right now clucking that I should be carrying my own reusable cloth shopping bags—I know that. As a matter of fact I do carry my own reusable cloth shopping bags. They're in my car behind the driver's seat. I always recall that they're in the car behind the driver's seat about the time the clerk is asking me whether I'd prefer paper or plastic.)

The salmon question is equally perplexing. Detractors claim the very idea of raising salmon in pens is insane. The fish, they say, are flabby, laced with antibiotics, riddled with sea lice and about as tasty as mulched telephone book. Said fishbots also pollute the seabed, consume outrageous tonnages of vulnerable fish foodstock and, by escaping from their pens, threaten to infect and/or mongrelize wild salmon stocks.

Fine, then. Let's just catch and eat wild salmon.

Or what's left of them. We're told that Pacific salmon stocks, from California to Haida Gwaii, are already seriously stressed. Atlantic salmon? It is to whimper. We fished those to death decades ago.

Of course with our federal government fisheries experts in charge, there's no way we could possibly be stupid enough to overfish the remaining wild salmon, right?

I've got four words for you: In Cod We Trust.

How about electricity? Well, those coal-fired generators sure work fine—aside from the noise and the air pollution. Hydro-generated electricity, then—you don't have to worry about dirty air with hydro—although you do lose the odd river system or two in the process.

Now, nuclear power . . . that's different. Nuclear's super clean. And quiet.

Of course, if something goes wrong, it gets real quiet. For about 250,000 years.

When it comes to the environment, nothing is as simple as it looks. Wind turbines looked for a while like a wonderful power alternative. Sure! Windmills! Non-polluting, silent—and what could be cheaper and more satisfying than harnessing the breeze?

But there's an aesthetic price. Tier after tier of what look like giant eggbeaters whirring away on a craggy bluff do not constitute a picturesque vignette. Plus there's the slice-and-dice effect those whirling blades have on migrating flocks of birds . . .

As Kermit said, it's not easy being green. And few bipeds know that better than Carolynn Bissett and Richard Treanor of Sunnyvale, California. Richard and Carolynn are dyed-in-the-non-synthetic-wool environmentalists. They recycle. They belong to the Sierra Club. They drive a Prius.

That's why they were shocked when they got the court order from the State of California ordering them to chop down the eight giant redwoods in their backyard.

Reason? The trees were casting a shadow on a neighbour's solar panels, rendering them useless. And in California, solar panels trump trees.

Hilarious? Not if you're Richard and Carolynn. So far they've spent more than $25,000 in legal fees trying to protect their trees.

When it comes to bedrock stupidity, one should never underestimate the boundless capacity of the human race. Environmental awareness is merely the latest frontier we have yet to plumb.

And we're already making important inroads. Not long ago, the media giant NBC flew its East Coast environmental correspondent, Anne Curry, complete with film crew, from the New York office all the way to the South Pole.

So that Ms. Curry could do a forty-five-second stand-up report.

On global warming.

IT'S YOUR FUNERAL . . .

*I could never bear to be buried with people to whom I
had not been introduced.*
    —NORMAN PARKINSON, BRITISH PHOTOGRAPHER

Unfortunately, most of us don't get to choose all of our next-door
neighbours in the Great Hereafter, but we do have some say
in how we present ourselves to them. Which is why I found myself
window shopping for wicker baskets last week. Found a beauty in the
house furnishings section down at Home Hardware. Nice and deep,
about three feet long and thirty inches wide, made of hand-woven
willow. It's on sale till the end of the month for only $19.95. I figured
I could buy a pair of them, glue them together end to end, knock out
the middle partitions and have myself a nifty little getaway pod (a.k.a.
coffin), all for less than fifty bucks.

A little morbid, you think? Hardly. Forward thinking, I call it.
There's a cemetery not far from where I live and (currently) breathe
that has already set aside a half acre of its premises to exclusively
accommodate 284 "eco-graves"—plots in which the environmentally
sensitive Newly Expired can pre-arrange to have themselves planted
in "biodegradable caskets."

Makes sense to me. I have never understood the peculiar penchant of my tribe for interring our departed in outrageous circus
floats hand-crafted of exotic woods, brushed silk and burnished
brass, the sole function of which is to transport said remains from the
funeral parlour to a hole in the ground, never to be seen again.

It is, perhaps, the ultimate in human folly. One last pathetic stab at immortality. Shakespeare recognized—and nailed the futility of it—more than four centuries ago:

Golden lads and girls all must

As chimneysweepers, come to dust

As I say, the wickerware casket makes perfect sense to me. What makes less sense is the fact that (a) Canadian law prohibits me from whipping up my own casket, DIY style, down in my basement; and (b) once I turn the project over to the professionals, I'm going to pay considerably more than the aforementioned half a C-note.

If, for instance, I engage the services of the Evergreen Casket Corporation, one of the world leaders in the biodegradable coffin game, I can expect to fork over a base price of $2,000 for a casket made of wicker (which, on their website at least, does not look a helluva lot more upscale than my fantasy Home Hardware jobbie).

Two thousand bucks? For a one-use-only takeout tote box made of dried grass? Such naked avarice would bring a blush of embarrassment to the cheeks of an oil company executive.

I could probably get myself a better deal if I lived in Europe. They ran out of cheap and vacant space for expired citizens centuries ago. Consequently, Europeans are much more open to cheap and efficient disposal options. Over there you can choose from a whole line of inexpensive caskets made of honeycombed recycled cardboard—even biodegradable urns. Hey, if I was lucky enough to kick off in India, I could have myself barbecued and pecked into the next world by vultures along the banks of the Ganges . . .

Yeah, well. Some options are just a little too cheap.

We're still getting used to the idea of economical, environmentally friendly burials on this side of the water. "Eco-burial," as it's known, is a fledgling industry in Canada—and our next-door neighbours are just as behind the times. Population of the USA: three hundred and ten million. Number of natural burial grounds: ten.

There's an old saying that the only things certain in life are death and taxes, but I'm not so sure about the first one. Even in death, you can't always get what you want. I'm reminded of the story of poor old Ben Jonson, a dramatist contemporary of Shakespeare. Ben, who thought he had the ear of King Charles I, asked for "just a square foot" in Westminster Abbey for his burial plot. King Charles either didn't like Ben much or else he had a wicked sense of humour. Visit Westminster Abbey and you can see Ben Jonson's grave. His gravestone is exactly one foot square and the remains of Ben are indeed beneath it. The king had him buried standing up.

IT'S NOT EASY BEING GREEN

It seemed like such a great idea. Inspirational, really. Landscape gardener Raoul Surcoul and physiotherapist Richard Spink, both dedicated environmental activists, had spent four years laboriously preparing a very special polar expedition that would feature solar panels and a cutting-edge wind turbine. Purpose: to achieve the first carbon-neutral crossing of the Greenland icecap in the history of the planet. One spring day they set sail—pardon me—they carbon-neutrally chugged out of Bristol harbour, England, in a welter of whirring TV cameras and media microphones. Twenty-five thousand British schoolchildren eagerly monitored their progress on-line.

Two days out of Bristol their boat foundered. Raoul's and Richard's dream went to the bottom of the sea; happily, their sorry butts were saved by a passing ship.

If nothing else, the abortive expedition kept one staunch human tradition alive. Whatever other challenges we face, we humans know that in the field of Environmental Screw-ups we as a species have no equal.

Back in the late 1800s a New York philanthropist had an inspiration: wouldn't it be glorious if all the wondrous creatures mentioned in the works of Shakespeare could find a new home in North America? Brilliant! He would start with . . . let me see . . . Yes! That beautiful iridescent bird of the English countryside—the starling. In

1890 the philanthropist arranged for a hundred European starlings to be released in Central Park.

Today the starling population of this continent has grown to more than 250 million. The bird's become the bane of other bird species and of North American agriculture, not to mention North American windshields and park benches.

We never learn. Years ago, some Aussie thought it would be fair dinkum to have rabbits Down Under, so he imported a few pairs. Australia got rabbits all right.

When I was a kid in Toronto, Canada geese were as rare as Stanley Cup parades. Forty years on, many parks in Hogtown are all but unwalkable, thanks to goose poop. Downtown traffic regularly grinds to a halt on Lakeshore Boulevard to allow waddling caravans of geese and their gosling broods to cross the road.

The only force likely to knock the Canada goose off its perch is its avian cousin, the cormorant. The snake-necked bird also used to be a rarity in the Great Lakes but no more. Cormorants have taken over—and pretty much destroyed—many swatches of the Great Lakes tapestry, including Middle Island in Point Pelee National Park, Lake Erie. Cormorants crap a lot. Nearly half the island's trees have been killed by a blanket of cormorant guano. The very chemistry of the soil has been changed. Can the island be saved? Park superintendent Marian Stranak has her doubts. She told a *Globe and Mail* reporter, "This is a dying island with a dying population of plants and animals."

Want to guess which species bears responsibility for the cormorant explosion? Decades ago, freighters and tankers from Europe introduced a whole new foodstock for the cormorant when they accidentally released scads of imported alewife fish from their ballast tanks into the Great Lakes. American fish farmers completed the smorgasbord by introducing farmed catfish in the cormorant's wintering habitat.

Ironically, we often do worse by trying to Do Good. Remember when the Everglades alligator faced extinction a few years back? US lawmakers sprang to the fore, banning hunting of the creature and the sale or even possession of alligator hides. The gators have rebounded nicely and are now picking off an average of a dozen humans a year. Remember when South Africa declared a moratorium on ivory merchandising back in the mid-nineties? The elephant population of Kruger National Park has now doubled and they're running out of food. Looks like the park elephants will soon face a grim choice: starve or be culled. "Culled" is a weasel word for "shot."

And let's not forget our own plains bison. Human rapaciousness almost wiped out that magnificent beast a century and a half ago. Hadn't been any in the Grasslands National Park area of Saskatchewan since the late 1800s (about the time Central Park was last starling-free). Recently, 130 bison were reintroduced to the park and they're doing splendidly. So splendidly that parks officials are already worried. "The area can only support so many animals," a parks spokesman says. "If there are more . . . they will graze the grass down to the dirt [until] there is actually nothing growing."

Trouble is, we've pretty much run out of suitable habitat to relocate the bison.

Robbie Burns said it well—the best laid plans of men, and all that. Remember that intrepid duo of environmentalists who sank their boat trying to become the first humans to complete a carbon-neutral crossing of the Pole? Guess what saved their bacon when they were bobbing, shipwrecked in the North Atlantic?

An oil tanker. Carrying 680,000 barrels of crude.

THE DEXTER: TOO CUTE TO KILL

Anybody remember the Shmoo?

It was a critter dreamed up by Al Capp, the cartoonist who created the *Li'l Abner* strip seventy-odd years ago. The Shmoo was about the size and shape of a bowling pin, except it had tiny legs, a perpetual grin and big friendly eyes. Shmoos ran in packs and liked to hang around with humans. They lived on air and water, liked to be stroked and fondled like puppies, but most of all, they loved to be eaten. Why, a Shmoo would jump right into the frying pan in anticipation.

Tasted like fried chicken, readers were told.

The Shmoo was a socialist's wet dream—a plentiful food stock that didn't have to be fed or stabled, cultivated or harvested, taken to market or slaughtered. Most of all, the Shmoo was a hot meal that didn't engender feelings of guilt or remorse in consumers. The Shmoos *wanted* people to eat them.

Mother Nature never did give us the Shmoo but she came tantalizingly close. Ladies and gentlemen, allow me to introduce the Dexter.

The Dexter is . . . well, let's call it a lawn mower. It runs very quietly, gets excellent mileage with minimal maintenance. The Dexter not only keeps your grass trimmed, it fertilizes it at the same time. And the Dexter uses no oil at all. In fact, it uses no gasoline. Or electricity, or batteries or solar panels.

The Dexter runs on—how cool is this—grass.

Big deal, you say. Goats and sheep can eat grass—hell, I've got deer in my yard that do the same thing.

Yeah, but can you get a quart of milk off them every day?

The Dexter is a cow. It moos like a cow, gives milk like a cow, eats grass and grows horns and has calves like a cow. The big difference between a Dexter and, say, a Holstein is that a decent milking Holstein is the size of a Dodge minivan. A Dexter is not much bigger than a Labrador retriever. A nasty-tempered or just plain clumsy Holstein can crush you like a grape against a stable wall. If it steps on your foot you won't walk for a week. Whereas Dexters are affectionate and almost small enough to pick up in your arms.

And unlike the Shmoo, the Dexter is real. It exists. It is a mountain breed from Ireland that has been around for ages and is now found on farms around the world. Last time I checked, more than 4,100 Dexter cows were registered by the Dexter Cattle Society.

A dozen or so of those cows live on the rolling fields of a twenty-acre farm belonging to poet and songwriter Pam Ayres, who lives in the Cotswolds in England. It's a family affair sans bureaucratic interference and that's just the way Pam Ayres likes it. "The government has no interest in where our food comes from or how it tastes," she told a *Sunday Times* reporter. "So it's nice to set your own welfare and quality standards."

The Dexter is just the opening wedge of the blooming mini-cow boom. The Australian government is getting involved in a big way. They've crossbred cattle strains to produce two new breeds—the Miniature Hereford and the Lowline Angus. The latter can produce 70 percent of the meat of its big sister, yet it stands only thirty-nine inches high.

So what's the big attraction? Economy of scale, for one thing. As any cattle producer can tell you, the cost of raising conventional cattle is going through the barn roof. Heating, transportation—and especially the cost of feed—are all escalating astronomically. Mini-cattle obviously take up less room and need way less fuel than their oversized cousins.

My hunch is that for some consumers these mini-breeds are going to cut out the cattle-producing middlemen entirely. If you've got access to a couple of acres of grass, why buy your milk and meat at the supermarket? You can raise it yourself. As one Dexter owner says, "As long as you've got plenty of grass they will be fine. You don't really have to feed them . . . and they have a lovely temperament."

Ah, there's the rub. These Dexters and Mini Herefords and Lowline Anguses are, when all is said and done . . . kinda cute.

I have a theory that if some future anthropologist could travel back in time and interview us, the conversation would go something like this: "Let me get this straight. You . . . *ate* . . . your fellow creatures? You actually raised animals, fed them and sheltered them and nurtured them, then you sent them off to abattoirs and slaughterhouses and you had them killed and dismembered and separated into gobbets of protein in shrink-wrapped packets on Styrofoam trays and you sat down and . . . *ate* . . . them?"

And we will say, "Well yeah, we did. Right up until the Dexters. That's when we all went vegetarian. Those Dexters were just too damn cute to kill."

MILES WIDE AND INCHES DEEP

Yoo-hoo . . . Hello?

Yes, I'm talking to you. Are you experiencing difficulty staying with this paragraph? Here's a suggestion: why don't you click off Peter Mansbridge, pull the iPod out of your earhole, turn your cell to vibrate and ignore your email for a nanosecond?

There . . . isn't that better?

This, believe it or not, is the way we all used to live. Peacefully, more or less. Meandering from one task to another in a linear, sequential, one foot after the other, Opie-sauntering-down-the-main-street-of-Mayberry kind of way—not trying to juggle eighteen things at once. Not driving ourselves crazy.

I'm not sure exactly when multi-tasking became the fashion, but it's not working that well for me and if I had my druthers I'd whisk us all back to those good old take-it-as it-comes days of yore.

Not working that well for most of us, apparently. Fielding a call from Aunt Agnes or checking the BlackBerry while tooling along in the passing lane on the Trans-Canada is a poorly concealed death wish at best, but multi-tasking bushwhacks us in dozens of less obvious ways. For one thing, it renders us dopier than, well, dope. A study carried out by the Institute of Psychiatry at the University of London concluded, among other things, that workers interrupted by email and phone calls "suffer a fall in IQ more than twice that found in marijuana smokers."

Plus, the thrill of that robot voice chirruping "You've got mail!" falls considerably south of the buzz from a bong hit.

And multi-tasking isn't just taking over the workplace. My folk-singer friend James Gordon recently had an eerie experience. He received an invitation to perform at a coffee house in Brooklyn, New York. Hot dog! he thought—the Big Apple! He showed up on the appointed date at Vox Pop, a hole-in-the-wall joint that billed itself as a "community-empowering, retail-revolution, live-event-loving infoshop." Hmm, thought my friend. But he unslung his guitar and took to the stage.

"I looked out into a sea of Mac PowerBooks," he recalls, "each one blocking out the faces of the pale patrons. It turned out that Vox Pop really was a place for lonely, anti-social computer geeks to sit by themselves at tiny tables, drinking coffee while immersing themselves in their laptops. They seemed genuinely annoyed that there was a noisy folksinger disturbing their peace."

Taking your laptop along as your date. When did this depressing cultural innovation raise its misanthropic head?

It would be excusable perhaps if multi-tasking worked. We could forgive the intrusion if all of our frenetic simultaneous hyperactivity actually put us ahead of the game and made us more efficient and knowledgeable, but it doesn't. We get to juggle more data, yes. But that's all it is—infobits that don't knit together into a cohesive whole. The upshot? Very fast results, but also very shallow. We end up being like so many isolated Lake Eries—each of us miles wide and inches deep.

Some experts think that multi-tasking is permanently recon-figuring our minds. A study conducted by Russell Poldrack, a psychology professor at the University of California, concludes that "multi-tasking adversely affects how you learn." "We have to be aware that there is a cost to the way our society is changing," says Poldrack. "Humans are not built to work this way. We're really built to focus."

Doesn't show any sign of letting up, though. Enter Twitter, a "social interaction service" now available to Internet uses everywhere. Twitter allows a user to keep in touch with fellow browsers *moment-to-moment*. The catch is, messages can be no longer than 140 charac-ters—which leads to scintillating conversations such as:

WATCHA DOIN?

NOT MUCH. YOU?

EATING LUNCH.

LATER, BRO.

There's an even newer program called Whisper that allows users to "gently interrupt" other users by sending a pop-up message to intrude on their screens. In case you weren't distracted enough already.

Tennyson would not be happy in these times. He's the guy who wrote: "There is no peace but calm." Not everyone would agree, of course. Someone else opined: "Mankind has grown strong through eternal struggles and it will only perish through eternal peace."

Chap named Hitler wrote that.

PAPERLESS SOCIETY? HAH!

The pen was an archaic instrument, seldom used even for signatures . . . Apart from very short notes, it was usual to dictate everything into the Speak-Write.
—GEORGE ORWELL, *NINETEEN EIGHTY-FOUR*

Ah, yes. According to Orwell's terrifying but, it turns out, not-so-prophetic novel, we should be into at least our third decade of the Paperless Society by now. Orwell predicted that it would be achieved through tyranny. Other Brave New Worlders among us have been forecasting the end of paper since at least the 1970s.

The forecasts were a tad premature. A poll released by Leger Marketing shows that we're using more paper than ever before. According to Leger, Canadians are printing out about thirty pages of documents per person, per day.

Like most polls, this one makes me scratch my head a bit. *All* Canadians? I certainly don't achieve that daily quota, and I seriously doubt that Nova Scotia lobstermen, BC tree planters and Manitoba canola farmers are downing traps, shovels and disc harrows to rush over to their printers and churn out thirty pages of data every day, but let it pass. This poll boasts a margin of error "plus or minus 3.4 percentage points, nineteen times out of twenty," and who am I to argue with performance figures like that—whatever the hell they might mean?

Let's suppose the poll is accurate. Let us further suppose the Leger pollsters are correct in their observation that nearly half the respondents are producing even more documents than they were five years ago. In other words, that the Paperless Society is getting further away rather than closer.

The pollsters report this as if it's some strange and inexplicable phenomenon. I say: "Yeah, so? What did you expect?"

People *like* paper. You can hold it in your hand or fold it up and put it in your pocket. Next time you check, the paper will still be there. It won't vanish in a phosphorescent poof, or greet you with a line of type reading "file not found" or "Internet access not available at this time."

And that's the other side of this two-faced socio-cultural shekel: as much as we feel comfortable with paper, we fear and loathe our computers. Why wouldn't we? Personal computers, once heralded as technological Lone Rangers riding to our rescue, have turned out to be tiresome and infuriating burdens ranking somewhere between migraines and jock itch.

The personal computer. Like brassieres that hook at the back, the Edsel and the notion to introduce rabbits to the Australian outback, it seemed like a good idea at the time.

But then hooking up with the Great White Gods From Across the Sea seemed like a good idea to First Nations people—until they found out about VD and smallpox. PCs, too, come with a blizzard of technological variations of the clap. They're even called viruses. My computer guru informs me that I need to make my computer password "more sophisticated" to foil hackers and the viruses they throw around like grass seed.

"You mean 'ablack44' isn't wily enough?" I ask her. She smirks. "Your password should be at least fifteen characters long," she tells me. "So . . . like 'Friendsromanscountrymen'?" I suggest. She smirks again. "Don't use a guessable phrase," she says. "Hackers love that. And be sure to throw in some numbers. And some upper and lower case. And some special characters."

I think we settled on "G%*rnxy*85thislAnd$&FnorZ" as my new password. I'm sharing it with you because I won't be using it. I threw up my hands when she told me I need at least four new passwords—and that I should change them all once a month.

Life's too short, folks. And paper's still too handy. Contrary to what Bill Gates told us, the personal computer is not "the magic key to the future." That was an empty promise.

As Sam Goldwyn said, "Never trust a verbal promise. A verbal promise ain't worth the paper it's written on."

THE SOUNDS OF SILENCE

Man has turned his back on silence. Day after day
he invents machines that increase noise and distract
humanity from the essence of life.

—JEAN ARP

It is very hard to find silence on this planet. I came close twice—once when I was several thousand feet under the earth in a hardrock mine in northwestern Ontario. The guy who was showing me around shut everything down—the elevator, the generator, even the carbon-arc lamps. Then he killed the ignition in the buggy we were riding in. That was pretty silent—but I could still hear my pulse.

The other time was scuba diving. Sixty feet under the waves with the Pacific Ocean pressing down on you is a pretty silent environment too—until you inhale. Drawing a breath through a scuba hose sounds like marbles rattling in an empty milk jug.

Fact is, total silence would creep you out and probably drive you bananas if you got too much of it. That's not likely to happen to any of us any time soon. Silence is a commodity that's vanishing faster than good manners and the polar ice cap.

Every morning I walk my dogs through a forest that is far from streets, houses, factories, schoolyards—all the usual noisemakers of modern life. But silent? Hardly. It's a cacophony of sound. The ravens croak, the chickadees tweet, the squirrels twitter, leaves flutter and the branches sigh and moan . . .

And that's all fine, of course, because those sounds are an

improvement on silence. They are the sounds that balm our nerves and medicate our frazzled souls.

Problem is, no matter how deep into the forest I go, I know that sooner or later other aural interlopers will bull their way into my earholes. Sooner or later I will detect the scream of a not-so-far-off chainsaw or the groan of a logging truck grinding its gears up Lees Hill. Or overhead I'll hear the thocketa-thocketa drum solo of a Sikorski helicopter ferrying a six-pack of Business Suits up the coast for a look at some marina/golf course development. And it's not just happening in my neck of the woods. Bernie Krause is an Australian who's been walking wilderness areas of the world for the past forty years. He doesn't take his dogs with him—he packs a tape recorder. Krause makes recordings of the wild sounds he hears out there and he's come to an alarming conclusion: not only are the wild sounds increasingly having to compete with intruding man-made sounds—they're losing the battle. And they are vanishing.

According to Krause, the random animal yips, bird songs and insect buzzings we hear in a walk through the woods are infinitely more complicated than we realize—and anything but random. He says it's more like a divinely orchestrated symphony. Krause creates spectrograms of his wilderness recordings. They are visual printouts that show all the "noises" of a given wilderness area arranged according to musical pitch.

It looks like an orchestral score—the woodwinds here, the horns over there, the strings off to the side. "No two species use the same frequency," says Krause. "That's part of how they coexist so well. When they give mating calls or warning cries, they aren't masked by the noises of other animals."

And when man joins the party? With his bells and horns and whistles, his grinding gears and thundering motors and wailing machines?

It's like a German oompah band crashing the London Philharmonic. Man-made noise jams the natural airwaves, cancelling out whole sections of the natural soundscape. Suddenly, entire species in a given area can no longer make themselves heard.

Krause says anthrophony—man-made noise—is wreaking havoc all over the world. Sometimes it's screamingly obvious—like squads of low-flying jets in training flights over Labrador traumatizing caribou herds. Sometimes it's not so obvious. Ever stuck your head under the water at the lake as a motorboat goes by? Imagine what seals and walruses, salmon and other fish stock endure with the marine traffic off our coasts.

When Europeans first came to these shores they caught cod off Newfoundland by simply dropping baskets into the sea. A century ago, passenger pigeons could block out the sun, endless buffalo blackened our plains and the noise of migrating whales kept Vancouverites awake at night. Now the Atlantic cod fishery is a fading memory, the passenger pigeon's extinct, the dwindling buffalo herds don't roam very far and the West Coast orcas are but the flick of a fluke away from a spot on the endangered species list.

That's not the kind of silence I crave.

IT'S A WEIRD, WIRED WORLD

I get up at 4:30 every morning. I like the quiet time.
It's a time I can recharge my batteries a bit. I exercise
and I clear my head and I catch up on the world. I read
papers. I look at e-mail. I surf the Web. I watch a little
TV, all at the same time. I call it my quiet time but
already I'm multi-tasking. I love listening to music, so
I'll do that in the morning, too, when I'm exercising
and watching the news.
— FROM A NEW YORK TIMES INTERVIEW WITH
ROBERT IGER, CEO OF DISNEY.

Bob? Hey, Bob? BOB!

It's me, over here. No, not on the phone, not on the screen, not at your door. In the flesh.

Got a news flash for you, Bob—that's not quiet time you've got going in the early hours of your morning. That's craziness. Craziness worthy of a cranked-up druggie on a methamphetamine run. You'll be lucky if you have a mental breakdown. It'll save you from a fatal cardio event.

It's no use. Bob's got his iPod buds screwed in deep and he can't hear a word I'm saying. Truth to tell, behaviour like Bob's, which only a few years ago would have earned a diagnosis of obsessive-compulsive disorder, is looking more normal all the time.

Consider a recent Apple iPhone application. Most of us have mastered the art of chewing gum while walking, but even the most technologically adept among us will recognize the challenge of simultaneously walking while tracking our email.

Well, stand easy, übergeeks. The folks at Apple have come up with "E-mail 'n' Walk." It's a package that takes a live feed from your phone's camera (you *do* have a working camera in your cellphone, do you not?), which is mounted on the rear of the device. This allows you to see what's in front of you *while you're walking and checking your email.* The text of your emails appears as white lettering superimposed on top of the video feed so that you can read the email at the same time you're dodging pedestrian traffic, garbage cans, dead pop tins and mounds of dog poop—brilliant, yes?

Er, no. Stupid, actually. But then I speak as an enthusiastic Luddite. I Twitter not. Neither do I Facebook, iPod or BlackBerry. I have a cellphone, yes, because I am approaching decrepitude and I still walk with my dogs in the woods each morning. If I fall and snap a femur I would prefer to be found before the snow flies. So I carry a cellphone, but only family members and my dog sitter know the number. As a matter of fact, I don't recall the number myself, though I'm sure I have it written down somewhere.

I resist full immersion in the technological tsunami because frankly, I don't have time—and I wonder where other folks find the hours to fritter away on tweets and blogs and all the other lame communication fartlets that bubble up unbidden about us. Christopher Moore thinks he knows. Moore is a BC novelist and he thinks the Web is a time vampire. He believes that entire books aren't getting written because would-be authors are AWOL, surfing the Internet. "I think that a lot of creative people want to be working on their craft, want to be thinking big about what they are doing [but] the culture is encouraging them to think small," says Moore.

Moore advocates a voluntary unplugging in order to get away from what he calls "the constant buzzing of the hive mind."

Naturally, Cyberworld has invented a program for that.

The program is called Freedom and it is designed to protect you from the Internet. Installed on your computer, Freedom can be set up to prevent you from emailing, surfing, browsing, on-line shopping and game-playing for periods of time ranging from sixty seconds to eight hours.

The idea is to free you from yourself—to give you some time away from mindless cyber browsing to actually do something creative.

I think Robert Iger, the Disney CEO, should install Freedom on his PC. Or he could try a program that's probably already installed in his home office. Next time he gets up at 4:30 in the morning, instead of turning on his PC and his TV and climbing on his stationary bike, Bob could go to the window and look east. See that big red ball on the horizon, Bob? That's the program's logo. It comes with a random soundtrack—robins, sparrows, crows, sometimes a dog bark or two. It's a cool program—no commercials, no virus alerts—and best of all, it's a free download!

Whaddya think, Bob? *Bob?*

It's no use. He's not listening.

HOW MUCH IS THAT IN WATER?

I was watching Craig Ferguson, the ex-pat Scots comic-turned-unabashed-American-flagwaver as he gently dissed Canada on the tube the other night. "To me," said Ferguson, "Canada is not the party. Canada is the apartment above the party."

Some truth to that. We Canucks are a tad stodgy—if you're comparing us to the East Village, San Francisco's Castro or Rodeo Drive. But if your American reference is Boise, Idaho, greater Wyoming or downtown Bubba, Texas, Canada is kilometres ahead on the hipster scale. We're Errol Flynn crossed with Frida Kahlo compared to most of backwater America.

H.L. Mencken was closer to the mark when he said: "Nobody ever went broke underestimating the intelligence of the American public."

Or so I used to think. A couple of stories in the news recently made me re-evaluate the transborder IQ comparison. The first story comes from the *Los Angeles Times*. It's headlined: "Americans Turn to Tap as Bottle Water Prices Get Hard to Swallow." The story relates how US consumers have finally twigged to the realization that bottled water is the biggest con since Enron.

Maybe bigger. Americans shelled out a jaw-dropping $16.8 billion for bottled water last year—this for a product they could get from the kitchen tap for free.

Okay, not for free, but for pennies a year. Anybody who gets their daily water intake in Dasani or Aquafina bottles is spending thousands of dollars annually.

For water.

And Americans have finally figured it out. They've realized that bottled water is not only no healthier than tap water, it *is* tap water in many cases. Dasani? Bottled by Coca Cola. Aquafina? Brought to you by PepsiCo. And both are drawn directly from municipal water supplies. People who drink Dasani or Aquafina get to pay for it twice—once through their taxes, then again at the checkout counter.

But Dasani and Aquafina are the McDonald's and Taco Bell of bottled waters. Consumers who are truly discriminating prefer premium brands, brands that might be distilled, decanted, oxygenated, de-ionized or even osmosis reversed. They may, their labels will claim, have been captured from remote glaciers, diverted from sparkling mountain streams or, as in the case of New Zealand's best-selling Eternal artesian water, "filtered through layers of volcanic rock where it has collected for a millennia [sic]."

Still just water, folks.

Not that you'd guess from the price tag. A single glass of Evian water at Claridge's in London will add five quid to your tab. You can pay $33.50 for two ounces of MaHaLo, a desalinated seawater brand bottled in Hawaii. (Mind you, that's a concentrate. You have to dilute it before you indulge. Which means you must add water to your, er, water.

But hell, let's assume you're a fabulously successful Colombian drug lord—or even a cabinet minister with a government expense account. In that case, you'll be wanting a chilled bottle of BlingH$_2$O sent over to your table. That really is the brand name and it really is available at finer watering holes everywhere.

It'll only set you back $480 for a special-edition 750-millilitre bottle. That's roughly a million times more than you pay when you draw the same product from your kitchen faucet.

But as I say, the Americans, those gullible souls, have finally figured it out. The worm has turned. The penny has dropped. They've seen the light.

Which brings me to the second news story that caught my eye. It's headlined: "Canadians Shun Tap, Turn to Bottled Water." The story is about a Statistics Canada survey that shows that three in ten

Canadian households reported drinking bottled water in their homes. Why? Safety? Few products are safer than North American tap water. As *Washington Post* correspondent Shankar Vedantam writes: "The supply of clean drinking water is an underappreciated scientific and technological achievement that rivals putting a man on the moon. Trillions of dollars have been spent to get clean drinking water to people at virtually no cost."

Taste? Tests have shown again and again that if you take away the labels most consumers can't tell tap from bottled water. Convenience? What can be more convenient than strolling to the kitchen sink, twisting your wrist and chugalugging as much as you want? Even Neil Rothwell, author of the StatsCan report, confesses to being buffaloed. "Something is driving these households to drink bottled water."

Now what could that be? Einstein famously said: "Only two things are infinite, the universe and human stupidity, and I'm not sure about the former."

Can I buy you a drink, Albert?

MONKEY SEE, MONKEY SKIDOO

A Superior Court judge in Quebec by the name of Hélène Langlois has closed a thirty-eight-kilometre snowmobile trail through the Laurentians. She also awarded millions of dollars in damages to all citizens living within a hundred metres of the trail. The decision leaves several thousand enthusiastic Quebecois skidooers all dressed up in their snowsuits with no place to go. It also sets an ominous precedent for the free and unrestricted movement of snowmobilers throughout the country.

It's difficult to know what to say in the wake of such a groundbreaking (snowplowing?) decision.

How about "Justice Langlois for Prime Minister"?

I never met the woman, but on the strength of her ruling, I'm elevating her to a front row seat in my pantheon of Canadian heroes. Right up there with Laura Secord, Charlotte Whitton and Stompin' Tom.

Understand that the trail Justice Langlois has closed to snow machines is no backcountry idyll. It was basically a snowmobile thruway for Montrealers anxious to escape from the city. It passed through neighbourhoods and by the homes of people who had moved to the country for peace and solitude.

Ask Normand Lacroix about peace and solitude. His house in Saint-Jovite is about sixty feet from the trail. "It was hell," said Lacroix. "There would be six hundred, seven hundred, even a thousand snowmobiles every day."

Well, no more. The route is closed. Monsieur Lacroix will now get the peace and quiet that every Canadian citizen should expect as a birthright, and if there's a God in heaven and she isn't wearing noise-suppression earmuffs, this decision will inspire lawmakers from Joe Batt's Arm to Bella Coola.

I can remember the time I saw my first snowmobile, many moons ago. I was making my way through an untracked stretch of deep, snow-laden bush in southern Ontario (yes, Virginia, there was a time when "wilderness" and "southern Ontario" did not constitute an oxymoron). It was a sunny day and the snow was deep, but the woods were ominously quiet with only the soft whump of my snowshoes disturbing the silence. Where, I wondered, are the birds? How come no zing-zing of pine siskins or rat-a-tat of woodpecker?

Then I heard why. The unmistakable snarl of snowmobiles labouring up a hill toward me. In a few minutes three machines appeared and wallowed past me belching and farting exhaust fumes and noise. Their riders looked at me as if I was a mildly curious rock formation. Nobody spoke. We couldn't have heard each other over the machines anyway.

It never seems to occur to snowmobilers that their pastime constitutes a gross invasion of everyone else's privacy plus a monstrous kick in the privates to Mother Nature. Their machines desecrate the winter peace and destroy the very pristine wilderness experience they purport to make accessible.

Sure, snowmobiles are important—even critical—to naturalists, law enforcement personnel, search and rescue teams and citizens who really need them. Fair enough. But the other 99 percent of snowmobilers? The parka'ed-up couch potatoes who would otherwise be slouched in front of the boob tube snorkeling taco chips and watching American football? The Canadian Council of Snowmobilers claims that snowmobiling is "great exercise." What exercise? Twisting a throttle? Zipping up a snowsuit?

The council also claims that snowmobiling "brings people outdoors to interact with nature." Well, yeah—and good luck, nature. Snowmobiles don't "interact" with nature—they gangbang it. On one Saturday afternoon recently scientists recorded higher carbon monoxide levels *at the west Yellowstone Park entrance* than you'd find on an LA freeway. In a single winter (1997) at the same park, snowmobiles emitted the equivalent of sixty-eight-years' worth of auto pollution. That's because those snowmobiles were lousily designed. They used a highly inefficient two-stroke engine that produced one hundred times more carbon monoxide and three hundred times more hydrocarbons than autos.

And that's without considering the noise pollution that drives me (and Normand Lacroix) nuts and does God knows what to wildlife. Listen: the greatest glory of this country's defining season is the peacefulness that winter brings. The ineffable calm of a landscape wrapped in a blanket of snow. And you don't need—in fact, you can't have—a snowmobile to enjoy that. Get a dogsled. Get some snowshoes. Get a pair of cross-country skis.

Get a life.

PART SEVEN

TAKING IT PERSONALLY

LET THE KIDS LIVE A LITTLE

Do you know where your kids are? You do? Then, quick—lasso and hogtie the little beggars, hose 'em down with hot, soapy water, muffle their bodies head to toe in bubble wrap and hide 'em in the attic. It's a jungle out there!

I'm serious. I have a report before me from the University of North Carolina warning about a kiddies' minefield that your offspring may be playing in right now.

Yes, I'm talking about "the beach." Did you know that beachgoers who innocently build sand castles or fill pails with beach sand are 13 percent more likely to suffer a stomach ailment—and 20 percent more likely to get diarrhea?

Are you one of those sun idolaters who mindlessly let their kids bury each other up to their nostrils in sand? Loser. The study says your kids have a 24 percent better chance of suffering gastrointestinal distress than that sensible family in their Sunday church clothes whose feet never leave the boardwalk. Meanwhile, your kids might as well be playing Russian roulette with a Glock 9 mil. As Chris Heaney, the study's lead author, so wisely warns us, "the beach is not a sterile environment." Who knew?

It's not just the beach of course. Kiddy traps lurk everywhere, just waiting to snare the unwary. That's why school kids in Chicago recently got to sit through a twenty-minute lecture on the dangers of the Hula Hoop. Meanwhile, an elementary school in Attleboro,

Massachusetts, has prudently banned the game of tag on school grounds because, as the principal points out, "accidents can happen."

He's right—and they can happen anywhere. That's why it's now possible to buy lid locks for your toilet seats (what if little Ashton or Kimberly fell in and drowned?). There is also a market for tiny gloves and mini-kneepads specifically designed to protect your wee ones during their first crawling experience across that perilous, hazard-strewn, bacteria-ridden war zone also known as the living room floor.

Just nutty Americans, you think? Think again. Recently the chief medical officer for the Vancouver Island Health Authority went public about the dangers of . . .

Roasting marshmallows.

Doctor Richard Stanwick counsels that children sitting around a campfire should:

1. Apply hand sanitizer before selecting a marshmallow;
2. Sterilize their roasting twig before impaling marshmallow thereupon;
3. Use clean tissue to carefully remove carbon from twig;
4. Put clean marshmallow on clean stick with clean hand and proceed.

Hold it! The doctor's not finished! He also warns to be wary of ingesting molten marshmallows. "If there's a flame coming out of it, it's probably too hot," he says.

Ya think, doc?

I'll tell you what Lenore Skenazy thinks—she thinks it's all paranoid bunk. Ms. Skenazy rocketed into the Parental Hall of Infamy a couple of years ago by allowing her nine-year-old son to ride the subway across New York City—gasp—*all by himself.*

The kid came through fine, but the mother was crucified in the media for her perfidy. Critics branded her "America's Worst Mom." Some recommended she lose custody of her children.

Ms. Skenazy's response? She snorted and flipped the flibbertigibbets a New York bird. In fact, she wrote a book called *Free Range Kids: Giving Our Children the Freedom We Had Without Going Nuts with Worry.* Our children, she writes, are a lot tougher and savvier than we give them credit for. She also points out that despite what we read and hear we are living in what is "factually, statistically . . . one of the safest periods for children in the history of the world."

Problem is, that's not what we're told when we open the newspaper, turn on the radio or watch the news at eleven.

Her advice is refreshingly common sensical: turn off the news, she says. Boycott baby knee pads. "Walk through the baby safety department of a store with your oldest living relative asking, 'Which of these things did you need?'"

Ms. Skenazy is right of course. She says it well, but a chap named Robert Cody said it best: "Have the courage to live," he advised. "Anybody can die."

He's right, too. You want security? Climb into a pine box. Get some friends to nail it shut and lower it six feet underground. Sprinkle liberally with sod—even beach sand if you like. You'll be absolutely safe down there.

MOTHER'S DAY - A MEA CULPA

There's a hoary old proverb that gets bruited about each year in early spring.

"April showers," the ancient adage goes, "bringeth forth May flowers."

That's not all that gets broughteth forth. In North America, the second Sunday of May is set aside to commemorate Mother's Day, an occasion which, if I dwell upon it too long, can still bathe me in a backwash of twitching self-condemnation.

My mother, bless her, has been gone almost thirty years now. Perverse as it may sound, there are at least two good things about that. Number one: I no longer have to feel quite so guilty on Mother's Day anymore. Number two: dear old mom doesn't have to find storage space for yet another crummy teacup.

Why the feelings of remorse? Because . . . well, hell—how do you ever pay back the person who Gave You Life? You love her, of course—but how could you ever possibly love such a paragon *enough*? How is it humanly possible to repay the one human in the history of human existence without whom you wouldn't even be, well, human?

For my money, the comedian Dennis Miller summed it up best: "You love your mother because she was your arrival terminal. She created you, so you always, always owe her and can never repay the debt. Being born is like asking Don Corleone for a favour."

Exactly. And how did I repay my mom each Mother's Day when I was a kid? With teacups. Each Mother's Day Eve, usually toward the close of the working day, I would scuttle down to Woolworths or Kresge's, find the china display and select, with careful reference to whatever remained of my weekly allowance, one cup and saucer. I usually chose Ornate Gothic—with fake gold piping and a purple floral pattern, if available. I would ask the salesperson to put it in a nice box. "It's for my mom—Mother's Day," I would simper. If I looked winsome and clueless enough they would sometimes even gift-wrap it for me.

She gives me life; I give her teacups. Aaargh.

Some kids, of course, grew up less wracked with Mother Guilt— Bernie Montgomery, for instance. Bernie and his mom had a different kind of a relationship: he was an only son; she was a complete and utter Gorgon.

"My early life was a series of fierce battles from which my mother emerged the victor," he wrote. "If I could not be seen anywhere, she would say, 'Go and find out what Bernard is doing and tell him to stop it.'"

A mother like that makes Life a tough lineup to crack, but Bernie Montgomery weathered the storm pretty well. He grew up to become Field Marshall Viscount Montgomery—Monty of Alamein to his generation.

But destiny is an equal opportunity bushwhacker and the Fates conspire to make sure Mother Guilt gets spread deep and crisp and even. Consider the case of Bob Feller. "Rapid Robert," with his blistering fastball and wicked curve, was the winningest pitcher the Cleveland Indians ever employed and he was in his prime that day in 1938 out there on the mound at Comiskey Park, mowing down Chicago White Sox batters while his proud and preening momma watched Her Boy from a prime, first-row seat along the first base line.

Could the potential for Mother Guilt atonement ever run higher? A mother's son pitching in a major league game? His mother watching from the stands? It's the top of the seventh inning. Chicago third baseman Marv Owen comes up to bat. Bob Feller stares, shakes off a signal from his catcher, winds up, pumps and hurls. Owen swings. The ball rips foul along the first base line.

Of course the ball arcs into the crowd. *Of course* it smacks an unwitting spectator in the head. *Of course* the unwitting spectator turns out to be Bob Feller's mom.

Mrs. Feller wound up with broken spectacles and a cut on the forehead. Her son Bob, devastated, stopped the game, sprinted over and hovered penitentially until the club doctor patched her up. Then Feller went back to the mound, picked up a new ball, glared lasers at Marv Owen and struck him out. Like a good mama's boy should.

Almost a storybook ending. About as good as Mother Guilt payback ever gets.

Certainly beats a crummy teacup.

LIES OUR PARENTS TOLD US

First it was one hour, then it stretched to two. I think it eventually got up to two and a half hours that we were forbidden to swim after eating. "Your guts will cramp up and you'll sink like a bowling ball," our elders assured us. Dutifully, we youngsters stayed out of the water, sweating like artesian wells until the requisite grace period had elapsed. Instead we played baseball, rode our bikes or ran around like mindless hyenas.

And one day it occurred to me: *How come I don't get stomach cramps playing baseball, riding my bike or running around like a mindless hyena?*

Because it was a myth. Swimming after eating doesn't cause cramps. Sure, you *might* get one. You might also get hit by lightning or adopted by Madonna. Swimming cramps was just one more Grim Fairy Tale that oldsters used to keep us kids in line.

There were lots of others. I had an aunt who used to bushwhack me at the back door when I was on my way outside to go tobogganing.

"Wear your toque and scarf," she'd thunder. "Or you'll catch your death of cold."

Wrong, auntie. Viruses, not temperature fluctuations, cause colds.

Lots of stuff would cause cramps, though, according to the gossip in the schoolyard. It was an absolute given that if you swallowed the stone from a fruit you were eating there was a better than even chance that a peach, cherry or apricot tree would soon be taking root just behind your belly button. And we all knew for a fact that it was madness to swallow your bubble gum—because it took gum *seven years* to dissolve in your stomach.

Speaking of assaults on the stomach, did you, as I did, wrestle with the next-to-impossible dictum that we all must drink eight to ten large glasses of water a day? I shudder to think what I put my kidneys through, trying to achieve that quota. Turns out to be another fairy tale. It's been around since the end of World War II but nobody knows who started it, and no credible authority thinks there's any truth to it. Barbara Rolls, a nutrition researcher with Pennsylvania State University says, "I have no idea where the eight-glasses-a-day rule came from—and I've written a book about water."

Guilt-inducing fairy tales are still a-borning. Have you noticed the proliferation of antibacterial hand sanitizers in hospital waiting rooms and doctors' offices? Big business. Sales of the germ-fighting gels have skyrocketed by 80 percent in the last little while. Hand sanitizers are so popular they've given rise to a brand new phobia that the experts have tagged with the memorable handle HSOCD. That stands for Hand Sanitizer Obsessive Compulsive Disorder. Increasing numbers of people are becoming obsessed with washing their hands forty or fifty times a day. Billionaire Howard Hughes had the same phobia. And don't forget: Howard Hughes was nuts.

Experts say that not only is excessive devotion to your hand sanitizer more than a touch anal, it probably doesn't offer you any real protection anyway.

Common sense would tell you that a tribe that's been around for a couple of hundred thousand years as modern humans have, probably doesn't need hand sanitizers to carry on, but common sense and folk mythology have different postal codes.

Take that other modern obsession: obesity. Everybody knows what causes fat bums, jiggly thighs and pendulous guts—it's that darned protein imbalance, right? No, wait—that was last month. You want to know why you can't do up your pants? Blame it on genetics, fast food or lack of exercise. You can also claim an adrenal disorder, metabolic irregularities or something truly exotic like gastroesophageal reflux. (I blame my big butt on polycystic ovaries.)

The truth, it seems, is somewhat simpler. A recent study conducted by the World Health Organization Collaborating Center for Obesity

Prevention concludes that the rise in obesity among Americans since 1970 "was virtually all due to increased energy intake."

Translation: people are fat because people eat too much.

Call me a cynic, but a multi-million-dollar study that tracks the eating habits of 1,399 adults and 963 children over a thirty-year period, only to conclude that we're fatter because we eat more than we used to, makes me feel like laughing like a hyena.

Which, by the way, they don't. Laugh, I mean. The weird noise hyenas make has nothing to do with having a good time. Sarah Benson-Amram, who spent two years studying hyenas in Kenya, says, "In fact, they're usually pretty stressed out. Often they giggle once they've been attacked."

Another lie our parents told us.

OBITUARIES? YOU BETCHA!

I have never taken anybody's life, but I have often read obituary notices with considerable satisfaction.
—CLARENCE DARROW

I'm not sure what it says about me, but I have a confession to make: I troll the obits.

I read the obituary columns in the newspapers pretty much every day. Not for pleasure, you understand. It's more like a racetrack tout perusing the racing form. I check first to see if anybody I know croaked overnight, and then I check to see if I'm older than the poor souls who actually did. Reading the obits is my way of finding out if I'm still staying ahead in the only competition that we all get to run in whether we're athletes or not—the Human Race.

A strange cultural accoutrement, your typical newspaper obituary. It frequently features a photo of the lately defunct, sometimes decked out in a kilt or a square dance costume, or perhaps wearing a party hat, arms fanned out around some buddies. Champagne glasses, Hawaiian leis and birthday cakes are sometimes in evidence. Often there's a big grin plastered over the dear departed's face—which begs the question: why is this person looking so pleased with himself? He's dead.

And that's when the realization hits you that almost nobody gets to choose the photo that goes on their exit visa—your successors (or some anonymous newspaper editors you've never even met) get to handle that grisly chore.

That, in turn, is what gives the obituary photos their peculiar, somewhat creepy resonance. The people photographed had no ink-ling that they were posing for their last public appearance.

You think my obituary fixation is a tad creepy as well? Hey, I'm but an innocent babe in the woods compared to Keith Anderson. In his day job, Anderson is a social work professor at Ohio State University but he spends his spare time combing the obituary pages of his local rag, the *Cleveland Plain Dealer*. And not just every after-noon edition. Professor Anderson has made it his business to peruse *the past forty years'* worth of *Plain Dealer* obituary notices.

Not surprisingly, he's noticed some patterns. One of the oddest is that, while people are living longer, their obituary photos are get-ting younger. He would occasionally come across a notice that would indicate a man had died at the age of, say, ninety-four, but the accom-panying photo would show a strapping young lad in a World War II army uniform.

Another photo would depict a winsome, nubile lass in her wed-ding dress; the actual notice would say that she'd been born in 1922.

Professor Anderson started to classify obituaries into a category he called "age inappropriate"—in other words, any picture that looked like it had been taken more than fifteen years before the person died. He found that back in 1967, about 17 percent of the photos accompanying death notices were age inappropriate. By 1997 the ratio had more than doubled to 36 percent.

Howcum?

The professor puts it down to society's ongoing love affair with youth. He thinks the people who choose the obituary photographs prefer to show the deceased at their so-called prime, rather than how they actually looked.

"As a society, I don't think we see someone who's eighty years old as at the prime of their life," he told a Canwest reporter, adding, "which is sort of ageist."

Yeah, sort of. We need to revamp our attitude about aging. As Captain Eddie Rickenbacker said, "If a thing is old, it's a sign that it was fit to live. Old families, old customs, old styles survive because they are fit to survive . . . Old-fashioned hospitality, old-fashioned politeness, old-fashioned honour in business had qualities of survival."

Applies to old-fashioned obituaries too. Back in 1891, the great showman P.T. Barnum was in ill health and realized he was on the way out. He was asked what his last wish would be. "I'd like to read my obituary," replied Barnum. The *New York Sun* granted his wish, running a four-column death notice exactly one day before Barnum died.

With, I'll bet, a smile on his face.

A ROSE IS A ROSE IS A ROSE - RIGHT, ROSE?

O, my Luve's like a red, red rose

—Robert Burns

A divine bonding, that. Poet, firebrand and skirt-chasing scally-wag Rabbie Burns, Scotland's greatest (some might argue *only*) gift to Romanticism coupled with the most romantic flower that ever bloomed—the cheerleader of the *Rosacea* family, the not-so-common rose.

I never appreciated the potency of the blossom until I bought a dozen long-stemmed beauties for my own Beauty, a few years back. Fate had me on a bicycle that afternoon, pedalling through town. I had to make a few stops on the way home and I figured a bundle of roses left in the bike's basket might prove too great a temptation for passing Lotharios, so I carried the bouquet with me, nestled in the crook of my arm while I attended to my chores.

I was treated like I was George Clooney.

Total strangers beamed at me and chortled heartily as if I was delivering winning lottery cheques. "Who's the lucky lady?" one asked. Others congratulated me, held doors open; one even patted me on the back.

Need I add that the smilers, congratulators, doorpersons and back-patters were all women?

A powerful botanical ambassador, the rose—especially when presented, with appropriate fanfare, by the fella to the lady.

There's a story about the French actor Paul Meurisse, a man renowned for being economical with his words—so economical he made Marcel Marceau seem like a babbling Rush Limbaugh. Once, smitten with a young demoiselle, Meurisse went into a Manhattan florist's shop, attracted by a legend in the window that read: "Say It With Flowers."

Meurisse prowled around the shop peering at every bloom. Finally he selected a single red rose and asked that it be delivered to the lady's address, accompanied by his card. "And is there any message?" asked the clerk. Meurisse thought for a moment, then took the flower and performed some artful pruning on the spot. He handed the face-lifted rose back to the clerk with a worried smile. "There you are," he said, "And even at that, I wonder if I haven't said too much."

I like to imagine what the young woman must have thought when she received Meurisse's card—along with a rose sporting only two petals.

Roses—even all-but-bald ones—speak volumes and they captivate the minds of lovers and thinkers alike. Shakespeare asked: "What's in a name? A rose by any other name would smell as sweet." And Matisse opined: "There is nothing more difficult for a truly creative painter than to paint a rose."

Even though it echoed in the first half of her surname, the flower held decidedly less mystique for Eleanor Roosevelt. The famous author, lecturer and wife of US president F.D. Roosevelt once told a reporter: "I had a rose named after me and was very flattered. But I was not pleased to read the description in the catalogue: 'No good in bed, but fine against a wall.'"

The only other rose story I know involves my uncle Vincent. Uncle Vince is getting on a bit and his memory, to be charitable, isn't what it once was. Last week he and his wife had another couple over for dinner. They're all pretty much old school, so after dessert, the men sat around the dining room table with cigars and coffee while the women retired to the kitchen. "Had a great restaurant meal downtown last night," Uncle Vince told his pal. "Can't recommend it highly enough."

"Really?" said the other man. "And can you remember the name of the restaurant?"

Uncle Vince knitted his brow, rubbed his jaw, squinted. "Oh, man," he groaned, looking up at the ceiling. "What's the name of that flower—you know—the red one? It's got thorns? You see it a lot around St. Valentine's Day."

The other man says, "You mean, the rose?"

"Yeah!" cries Uncle Vince excitedly. Then he turns around in his chair and yells into the kitchen: "Rose, what was the name of that restaurant we went to last night?"

A HORSE IS A HORSE,
OF COURSE, OF COURSE

Do you have an Inner Animal? Of course you do—we all do. Sometimes it's just a little tricky to figure out which animal it is. Pierre Trudeau was a slam dunk—a Siamese cat. Or perhaps a wolf. Paul Martin was more of a beagle. Don Cherry? Junkyard dog.

Some professions have honorary Inner Animals. Judges get owls; policemen get bulldogs; politicians get weasels.

Lawyers? That's too easy.

I, too, have my Inner Animal. His name is Shane. He is a buckskin palomino maybe fourteen hands, not real high, but stocky. I first met him when I was just a pup and Shane was not much more than a big colt himself. I remember our first encounter well. I grabbed a big tuft of sweet green grass and walked up to Shane, proferring my gift. He swung his great head down, chuffed noisily, then whisked my grass bouquet out of my hand. I stood there while he ate it down. Then he swung his velvety muzzle over my head and began to snuffle in my hair.

"He likes me," I shouted excitedly to my friends.

Then Shane lifted me off the ground. By my hair.

It hurt quite a bit, but it was at least a frank introduction to Shane and his wily, unpredictable ways. He was a horse you could never take for granted. And he was always testing, testing.

I remember the time a farrier was cleaning out Shane's front hooves. He had the horse's left front foreleg securely between his thighs, and he was facing astern. This is the classic farrier position for cleaning front hooves. The horse is effectively immobilized by having one foot off the ground. In such a position there's nothing the horse can do to retaliate or resist.

Usually.

Shane waited until the farrier was thoroughly engrossed in his chore, then leaned over and gracefully bit the farrier's ear.

Horses don't bite people on the ear. Shane did.

The expression "pushing the envelope" was invented for Shane. He could always surprise you, no matter how familiar you thought you were with him. I looked after Shane as I was growing up, feeding him, bedding him, grooming him. I figured we were pretty good pals. Then one day when I was shovelling out his stall I got a little impatient because he wasn't moving over fast enough to suit me. I gave him a little bunt in the haunch with the handle of my manure fork.

I can still summon up the vision of that rear hoof whizzing by at eye level just millimetres from my head. It was one of the few times Shane missed.

We could never figure out where Shane got his attitude. He wasn't a stallion, but he acted like one. Put him in with a herd of strange horses and in no time he was in charge, rounding up the mares, bossing the foals around and settling the hash of any other males who dared to question his kingship.

Then there was our personal moment of truth. It was a sunny winter afternoon. I had finished mucking out the stalls. Shane was outside in the corral. What a perfect day to ride him—bareback.

He bucked me off twelve times and I only lasted that long because there was a foot of snow on the ground and the landings were relatively soft. Weird enough that I kept coming back for more—Shane did too. He would actually come and stand in place so that I could mount him more easily—and he could buck me off again.

The thirteenth time I climbed aboard he was as gentle as a hamster and sashayed me around the corral like I was driving a Cadillac. I don't know if he was tired or bored or just being careful not to discourage me from future exciting afternoon outings. You could never be sure of much of anything with that horse.

Our lives diverged and I lost track of Shane. I heard he got sold a couple of times, finally ending up on a dude ranch riding stable north of Toronto. The very last thing I heard came from a cop I knew who told me about his weirdest emergency call—a buckskin palomino leading a herd of horses down Highway 27. "Damndest thing," the cop said. "Most horses jump over fences to get away, but this palomino, he just went around leaning his big bum against the rails until he found a weak spot. Then he not only escapes, he takes the whole herd with him. It was like a prison break."

Had to be Shane.

KNOCKING BACK EGGNOG

Cheers, everyone! I am just embarking on my third year without the lubricating accompaniment of alcohol—and frankly it hasn't been all that tough. Oh, booze and I were a hot item for years, but there comes a time in a lot of relationships when one of you looks across the pillow or the dance floor—or the rim of a wineglass—and realizes: "You know what? This ain't fun anymore."

So far, not drinking has been strictly a losing proposition for me. I lost twenty-five pounds, the blear in my eye, the fog in my brain and my visceral hatred for alarm clocks.

Pretty smooth sailing—but there is one time of year that's a bit sticky for non-drinkers. Christmas and New Year's. Hanukkah. Yuletide. Kwanza. Whatever you call it, it slides through all of our lives tumultuously and inexorably, gliding on a veritable Niagara of hooch.

Booze is everywhere and virtually everybody drinks at that time of year. Heck, my abstemious Aunt Beulah has her annual bumper of sherry every New Year's Eve while we crowd around the TV to see if Times Square technicians can jump start Dick Clark one more time.

There's even a dedicated libation for the season. Does anyone drink rum and eggnog at the cottage? On a picnic? After the Grey Cup parade? Of course not. You drink rum and eggnog in the stretch around Christmas and then you never hear of it until the next Christmas rolls around.

And people *want* you to drink the rum and eggnog. They expect it. Refusing rum and eggnog is kind of like repudiating Dickens or blaspheming Santa. It's not done.

"How do you want your eggnog, Buddy? Little nutmeg? How about a cinnamon stick in there?"

"Ah, no . . . just the eggnog please and, ah . . . no rum."

"NO RUM??? WHADDYA MEAN, NO RUM!"

Last year, though, resisting the rum and eggnog wasn't much of a challenge because I was too busy during most of the holidays. Busy with the snow dump. Then busy with the snow dump on the snow dump. And the power outages. And the dead telephone. And the downed Internet. And the non-delivery of newspapers and mail for five days. And the rain that followed the snow dumps. And the ice build-up in the eavestroughs that followed that.

I've never actually seen rain come directly through the ceiling before.

What with being snowed in, iced over and rained on, dodging rum-laced eggnogs at seasonal shindigs was the least of my problems.

Ah, but it was all worth it on Christmas morn, which dawned bright and dry. I lay in my bed thinking peaceful thoughts, listening to the dogs on the floor snoring softly. As Christmases go, it wasn't so bad, I thought. Only five, maybe six near-disasters. But that's over now, and here I am, with the sun shining through the window, the birds twittering in the cedars . . .

And with just the vaguest, slightly unpleasant aftertaste of—what is that? Oh, yes, eggnog—in my mouth.

Which is when I realized that I had mere seconds to get to the bathroom before I would become violently, spectacularly ill. In Technicolor.

Let us draw the curtain of propriety on the rest of that particular Yuletide surprise. I will just say that not only was I sick, I was ricocheting-off-the-walls dizzy. Too dizzy even to rise from my place of worship at the porcelain altar for, oh, forty minutes or so. So I lay on the tiles and pulled the bathmat around my shoulders.

I was actually feeling much better by the time the doctor arrived a few hours later. "Sounds like food poisoning," she said. "What did you have last night?"

"Well, eggnog," I said.

"Aha!" she pounced, making a six-gun with her thumb and fore-finger and metaphorically popping me between the eyes. "Did you have it with rum?"

No, I said. Just eggnog.

"Too bad," said the doctor. "Rum would have killed the bacteria."

THE ART OF LIVING
DANGEROUSLY

I'm thinking of branching out into a different kind of writing. I want to write a kids' book. Actually, a book just for male kids, to be precise. I've already got the title. I'm going to call it *The Dangerous Book for Boys.* It'll be full of detailed instructions that'll show young lads how to get involved with all kinds of risky, possibly blood-spilling activities. Things like building rafts . . . making slingshots . . . how to construct a go-cart . . . how to skin a rabbit . . .

You think the Canadian public is ready for a book like that?

Are you kidding me? Canadian *publishers* aren't ready for a book like that. Number one, it's sexist since it excludes half the human race in its very title. Number two it's . . . well, it's just entirely too dangerous, my dears. We live in an age when children are told not to run during recess; when jungle gyms are being removed from schoolyards to save our little darlings from the ghastly trauma of scrapes and bumps. Why, last year three public school kids in Nova Scotia were expelled because they showed up at their school with snow on their jackets. Clear evidence that they had been roughhousing in a snowbank. We will have zero tolerance for that kind of perilous nonsense, thank you very much.

A book like I'm proposing? Pah. I'd have platoons of politically correct commandos on my neck in a nanosecond. I'd be crucified, tarred and feathered, drawn and quartered, ridden out of town on a rail and probably microwaved in effigy in the teachers' lounge. Only question would be: in what order?

Nope. Nobody in this country would touch a book like that with barbecue tongs.

Which is a pity, because *The Dangerous Book for Boys* got published in Britain a few years back—and became a runaway best-seller. And it really does tell boys how to skin rabbits, build go-carts, make slingshots—and much, much more.

It was written by two brothers, Con and Hal Iggulden, with no encouragement whatsoever from publishers and an equally frosty shoulder from the British educational community. But the Iggulden brothers knew what kind of a book they wanted to write—the kind of instruction manual they would have killed to get their hands on when they were young boys.

And the book's a delight—even for those of us well past our short-pants-and-brush-cut days. Here for instance, is what the authors insist "every boy should have to hand":

- Swiss Army knife—to remove splinters
- Handkerchief—doubles as a sling
- Needle and thread—to sew up wounds, mend torn shirt
- Pencil and paper—to note down criminals' licence plates
- Torch (flashlight)—to read secret plans at night
- A marble—a big one, for luck

Strange thing is, when I was a kid, I don't think *The Dangerous Book for Boys* would have been such a hot seller. Why? Because we actually did most of the things it recommends. We made our own rafts and go-carts and catapults and bows and arrows.

What happened?

Television happened. Packman and Super Mario Brothers happened. YouTube and MySpace happened. Political Correctness and frivolous lawsuits happened. Pity.

If I had to use one word to sum up the Iggulden brothers' advice for boys it would be: *Move!* Get involved. Be active. Get off your pudgy, passive, pre-pubescent butts and *do* something. "Play sport of some kind," they write in *The Dangerous Book for Boys*. "It doesn't matter what it is as long as it replaces the corpse-like pallor of the computer programmer with a ruddy glow."

"You have to let kids take some risks," says Conn Iggulden. "If you don't they'll end up as some dreadful, pallid things without any spirit or courage."

And even though the book is directed exclusively at boys, it contains one chapter devoted to that scariest of all young boy challenges.

Girls.

"Treat girls with respect," says the book. "Remember they are as nervous around you as you are around them—if you can imagine such a thing."

Wish somebody'd taught me that when I was a boy. But then I wish I'd learned a lot of things you find in this book: five important knots . . . how to use your wristwatch as a compass . . . how to make invisible ink . . .

The magic ingredient for that last one? Urine.

Don't worry, ladies . . . it's a boy thing.

A TALE OF TWO PARROTS

Ever come across a book you *wish* you'd read? Happened to me last week. The book is called *Breaking Bad Habits in Parrots*. I wish I'd read that book twenty-five years ago.

That would be just before I laid out six hundred bucks for Sydney, a blue-fronted Amazon. Sydney, the pet-store owner assured me, would prove an affectionate, intelligent and altogether heart-warming pet.

The pet-store owner lied. Sydney was a feathered fiend. A winged wolverine. An avian Antichrist. "Sydney"??? His name should have been Satan.

Sydney had three prevailing habits. He shrieked and shredded and shat indiscriminately—frequently all three at once. He shrieked when he was in his cage; when he was let out of his cage he destroyed everything he could put his beak to, and that which he couldn't besmirch he be-guanoed with gusto. When I began to entertain fantasies of grabbing Sydney by the neck with one hand, my twelve-gauge Remington with the other and taking both out on the front lawn for a spot of impromptu skeet-shooting, I knew it was time to divest myself of Sydney in favour of a more benign animal companion, such as—oh, I don't know—a rabid wharf rat, perhaps? A black mamba?

Sydney went back to the pet store, the owner of which refused to give me my money back. I didn't mind. Knowing he would probably spend the rest of his life with Sydney was recompense enough.

It was just the luck of the draw, I guess. If I'd been hanging around a pet shop in Stamford, Connecticut, back in 1977 I could have shelled out a few bucks and bought Alex, a one-year old African grey and possibly the smartest parrot the world has ever known.

Scratch that. Alex *became* the smartest parrot, etc., thanks to Dr. Irene Pepperberg, a Harvard scientist. She bought Alex, and over the next thirty years she taught the bird to describe objects, how to make his desires known—even how to ask questions.

In doing so, Dr. Pepperberg turned the science of animal linguistics on its pointy little head. Until her experiment with Alex came along, most researchers had concentrated on trying to teach chimpanzees and monkeys how to speak because, well, they're more like us, right? Closer on the evolutionary scale and all that. Only problem is, as much as simians resemble us, their vocal chords simply aren't up to the job of reproducing human speech.

Whereas parrots can at least, well, "parrot" what they hear, be it a ringing telephone, a barking dog or human speech.

But Dr. Pepperberg took linguistic ability in animals to a whole new level. She proved that not only could Alex talk like a human—he could think.

By his mid-twenties (still young for a parrot) Alex could identify and name fifty different objects. He could also name their colours, their shapes and even the materials they were made from. He understood concepts such as "bigger" and "smaller," could count up to six—even appreciated the concept of "zero."

And he had personality to burn—including a finely honed sense of mischief. Once, at a press conference, Dr. Pepperberg struggled to get Alex to vocalize the shape and colour of an object she held in front of him.

Alex snootily ignored her, and the crowd of reporters grew restive. Desperate to give the press something to write about, Dr. Pepperberg left the stage to bring on another African grey, hoping the presence of another bird would stimulate Alex to "open up." As soon as she had left the stage, Alex looked at the audience, leaned into the microphone and murmured quietly, "Triangle. Purple."

Just how smart did this birdbrain get? Smart enough to have a vocabulary of 150 words; smart enough to ask for specific objects— and to reject items that were not what he asked for.

On the evening of September 6, 2007, as Dr. Pepperberg prepared to leave the lab, she bid Alex good night.

"You be good," said Alex. "I love you."

"I love you too," said the professor.

"You'll be in tomorrow?" asked Alex.

"Yes," said the doctor. "I'll be in tomorrow."

Dr. Pepperberg would, but Alex would not. He died in his cage that night, of natural causes. He and Dr. Pepperberg had had their last conversation.

I'd tell you about the last conversation I had with my parrot, Sydney, but this is not an X-rated book.

YOU'RE ON TV - BE COOL

The thing about going on television is . . . you've got to come off as cool, right? Nobody wants to flip on their TV and see some awkward, flustered, stammering goofball who looks like he just fell off the back of a rutabaga truck. So when my publisher's PR representative called to tell me she'd arranged an appearance on Toronto's number one morning TV show, I handled it smoothly.

"I'm hep to that jive," I assured her.

I showed up bright and early and got ushered onto the set—a huge open room with a ceiling full of klieg lights, a couple of TV monitors, a predatory-looking camera on wheels and a crew of half a dozen, all of whom were younger than me.

By a factor of about three decades. They talked knowledgeably about phenomena called Jay-Z and Rihanna. They used the word "dude" a lot.

Be cool, I told myself.

I was approached by a kid wearing headphones and carrying a clipboard in one hand and my latest book in the other. "You've been on with us before, right?"

"Yo, dude," I assured him.

"Who interviewed you last time? Was it Dina? Or Kevin? Or Manjit?"

I utter my first stammer. Fortunately the guy is a multi-tasker. He doesn't wait for my reply but introduces me to a woman named Gina, who is about twenty-five but looks very, as the kids say, simpatico. She's wearing glasses and a floppy cap and a ponytail.

Cool! None of your plasticized, big-hair TV Glitzeratti here. "I know it wasn't you that interviewed me," I say to her cleverly. "I would have remembered you." Gina and Clipboard Boy look at me oddly. Turns out Gina is the camera person. "Why don't you get yourself a cup of coffee," suggests Clipboard Boy, shepherding me away from the set, a smidgen of concern in his voice. "It's a single-cup espresso machine but the coffee is excellent. Just follow the instructions."

The instructions are in Italian. I punch a couple of buttons without much hope. Hissing and spitting ensues. Hot water begins to splash onto the floor. One of the crew glides over, shuts off the water, inserts a coffee bag and—oh, yes—a cup. "You looked like you could use some help," he murmurs.

Be cool, I remind myself. What I need to do is demonstrate by my body language that I am in fact, very relaxed and in-sync, TV-wise. What would George Clooney do? I ask myself.

Between me and the actual interview table is another table with a hot plate in the middle. This table is festooned with sticks of fancy bread, bunches of grapes, a couple of pineapples and various bottles of cooking stuff. It's for the cooking segment, in which a couple of chefs from a five-star hotel whip up some gourmet goodies on camera. The chef segment comes after me, so casually—sexily, even—I lean against the table to sip my espresso the way I imagine George would do it.

The table is on rollers.

The chefs go ballistic of course—they're *artistes*—but the pineapples that bounced across the set don't actually get in the shot, so viewers at home are none the wiser.

And it turns out the table caster didn't even break the skin on Gina's ankle so no real damage done, even though she put on this bogus woe-is-me limp. The coffee stains on my pants? No problem—they'd just shoot me from the waist up. I wasn't sure we could trust Gina with that as she'd be working the camera but I was in no position to object. By now the entire crew was following me with their eyes and a big guy I hadn't noticed before with SECURITY on his shoulder flashes seemed to be hovering wherever I went. Clipboard Boy was treating me with that exaggerated wariness bartenders reserve for surly drunks and customers who look like they might be carrying a knife. The makeup woman approached me like Indiana Jones entering the tiger's cage. She made a couple of half-hearted feints at my nose with her makeup brush then backed away.

I said, "What about my head? I'm bald!"

"Wear your hat," she advised.

What with the last-minute instructions about not talking to the camera, not fiddling with my hands and not hitting the microphone attached to my lapel, I don't remember much about the interview itself, except that it seemed to be over almost as soon as it started. Truth to tell, Gina distracted me with her scowl and fake limp.

"That was fun, dude," I enthused to Clipboard Boy. I tried to high-five him but Security Guy misread the gesture and went into a kind of kung fu stance. Clipboard Boy waved him off and walked me to the door. "We have to, like, do this for my next book, bro," I said.

Clipboard Boy said they'd be in touch.

SO YOU WANT TO BE A WRITER

Thumbing through this week's issue of the *Manchester Guardian* I come across this whimsical headline: "Why Not Be a Writer?"

It's an advertisement from a British company that claims it can make you a published author. You send them money and they will give you tips and shortcuts that will have you hob-knobbing with Alice Munro and Stephen King before you can say *Roget's Thesaurus*.

And really—when you think about it—why not? Being a writer isn't like being a structural engineer or a biophysicist—or even a long-distance truck driver or a TV repairman. You have to go to school to get those jobs. You have to take examinations and pass rigorous tests.

On the other hand, anyone can be a writer. All you have to do is . . . write.

Right?

It's curious how many people think being a writer is as easy as putting on a different pair of shoes. Such folks would never dream of trying to pilot an airplane or run a restaurant without first racking up years of schooling and on-the-job experience. But give them a Bic to flick and they reckon they're on their way to a Giller nomination.

There is the famous story of a neurosurgeon accosting Margaret Laurence at a cocktail party:

"So you're a writer, eh?" the brain surgeon says. "I plan to take up writing when I retire."

"What a coincidence," purrs Laurence. "When I retire from writing I plan to take up brain surgery."

"Why Not Be a Writer?" the headline says. I'll tell you why not to be a writer. You'll probably starve to death, for starters. Sure, authors like Margaret Atwood, Peter C. Newman and Alice Munro don't exactly have to take in boarders to pay the mortgage, but they, my friends, are the overachievers, the Great Blue Whales in the literary goldfish bowl. The rest of us guppies live on scraps. The truth is, most Canadian writers can't make a living wage from writing. They have to hold down outside jobs as teachers or writers-in-residence. Or cab drivers. Okay, you say, but that's novelists. Everybody knows most novelists starve in garrets. What about freelance journalism?

Hah. If it's money you want, become a bartender. Or a bouncer. Or a bookie. The odds are you'll make a lot more dough than the typical Canadian freelancer. The going rate for most freelance magazine and newspaper writers in Canada hasn't changed since the 1970s. That is not a typo. Most Canadian freelancers haven't had a raise in over forty years. And the going rate was no hell back then.

You probably think I send my chauffeur down in the Bentley to pick up my stipend for writing this book.

Hear that high, keening wail in the background? That's my publisher, laughing hysterically.

Mind you, it's not all sackcloth and ashes. Writing has its up side. The hours are flexible, there's no dress code and a significant proportion of the populace believes that if you are a writer you must be . . . deep.

There's that high, keening wail again.

No, wait—that's my wife.

The truth is, being a writer isn't a career option to be weighed against other employment opportunities like furniture refinishing or gunsmithing. Writers don't have much choice. We write because we have to. We may end up with a desk full of unpublished novels and enough rejection slips to paper the Calgary Saddledome, but we will continue to write—even if we have to take jobs as fruit pickers or pop bottle recyclers to pay the bills. Writing is what we do. Whether we're any good at it is pretty much beside the point.

As for shortcuts and hot tips on how to succeed at writing, the British author Aldous Huxley offered the best advice. Years ago, a young hopeful cornered him at a party and asked him how one became a writer.

"It's simple, old chap," said Huxley. "First go out and buy yourself quite a lot of paper and a bottle of ink and a good sturdy pen.

"There now! All you have to do is write!"

HOW I BECAME A RICH GUY

You probably don't realize it, but you are reading the words of one wealthy dude. I Am Loaded. Extremely well off. Filthy rich, even. Nobody asks me how I achieved my fabulous financial prosperity but if somebody did, I would tell them I became rich by following the example of another man of magnificent means, Aristotle Onassis.

You've heard of him? Greek shipping tycoon. At twenty-two he was a penniless refugee; when he died, aged sixty-nine, in 1975, his empire was worth half a billion dollars. Someone asked Onassis the secret to his success. He said he was rich because he wore no topcoat.

"Since I am known as a 'rich' person," he explained, "I feel I would have to tip at least five dollars every time I check my coat. On top of that, I would have to wear a very expensive coat, and it would have to be insured. Added up, without a topcoat I save over twenty-thousand dollars a year."

Exactly. That is also the secret of my success. I don't mean that I don't wear a topcoat; I just mean that I, too, am cheap.

Smoking? I gave that up years ago, but I was once a pack a day man. Last time I checked, smokes were selling for ten dollars a pack. I save $3,700 a year right there.

Gave up booze, too. Used to drink wine, beer on a regular basis and a martini from time to time. Doesn't take long for that to add up. Let's say I drank two bottles of wine, a half-dozen beer and one martini (a martinus?) every seven days. That's got to be a minimum of fifty bucks. *A week.*

Now, cranberry and soda is my social beverage of choice and I'm no longer shelling out at least $2,600 a year. If you throw in the tabs from parties, weddings and showers, expensive cab rides and drunken over-tipping I've got to be pocketing an extra four grand a year—just from not drinking.

We used to be a two-car household, but we sold one ($30,000) and replaced it with a motor scooter ($3,000). Savings: another $27,000. Used to cost me close to a hundred bucks a week to fill the tank on the old gas-eater. My scooter takes about five dollars every week and a half. Chalk up another $5,000 or so I'm saving every annum.

Vacations? I save a bundle there. I stay home. I don't go to the States anymore because . . . it's the States. Their economy is worse than ours and crossing the border is unpleasant and demeaning. Europe and Mexico are: (a) hideously expensive; and (b) dodgy in the food and mugging departments. Besides, you still have to face the customs goons when you come back. If I wanted to be abused and mistreated by anonymous, unsmiling thugs I'd just go down to the local Hell's Angels clubhouse and kick over a Harley. Much cheaper—and no passport required. So, by not going abroad I save at least four or five thousand a year.

Recreation? I don't live close to any major hockey, baseball or football franchise, so no overpriced season's tickets for me. As for personal sports involvement, hey, I'm an old guy. Nobody's going to sell me a $5,000 mountain bike, a Kevlar kayak or a set of skis to do the black diamond runs at Whistler at my age. I don't have the plaid slacks (or temperament) for golf and I'm too young for lawn bowling. Gotta be pocketing at least another ten or twelve grand a year there.

And I don't buy toys—well, not the expensive ones anyway. Don't have a BlackBerry, an iPhone, a GPS thingummy or a shuffleboard-court-sized plasma TV screen for my living room wall. Another ten thou a year I don't have to spend.

I'm retired, so I no longer have the expense of commuting to work—that also means my wardrobe expenses have plummeted. I dress for comfort now—sweatpants, T-shirts, running shoes. My business suits, leather shoes, ties and dress shirts? All gone to the thrift store—whence cometh aforementioned sweats, Ts and sneakers.

The money this saves is difficult to calculate, but let's round it off at $10,000 a year.

I don't play poker or the ponies and I don't buy Irish Sweepstakes tickets or patronize casinos.

Lottery tickets? Please. Do I look that dumb?

A retiree pays a lot less income tax than a working stiff. I save a huge wad there.

Granted, I no longer cash a weekly corporate paycheque, but who cares? Look at the money I saved in the past twelve months by not smoking/drinking/driving a Hummer/going abroad/holding down a day job/buying titanium golf clubs/playing roulette/wearing dopey white nipples in my ears.

Easily over $100,000. Makes me feel smug, fulfilled, holier-than-thou and fiscally astute, all at once. Just one question.

Where's the money?

WRITE THE #@*%ING LETTER

You down in the dumps? Burned out? PO'd and KO'd by the Long-Time-No-Sunshine Blues (also known as Seasonal Affective Disorder and/or Living Through a Canadian Winter)?

I can help.

I know how to make you feel better almost instantly—and it doesn't involve diet, exercise, prayer, shaving your head or ingestion of drugs, prescription or otherwise. All you have to do is respond in a positive way to the following mantra:

Write the #@%ing letter.*

You know the letter I mean. The one you should have written months—maybe years—ago. The one you've been putting off because the time's not right or you're way too busy or you can't find any decent paper, or, or . . .

It's just too hard.

Solution? Sit down and write it. Today. Now. You'll feel better, I guarantee it.

And that's not just me talking off the top of my head. Steven Toepfer, a professor at Kent State University, recently conducted a study into what makes people feel genuinely happy. He had a hunch the solution would involve gratitude, so he instructed his students to write one letter every two weeks to someone—anyone—who had had a positive influence on their lives.

The only guidelines were that the letters had to be positive, had to include some insight or reflection (in other words, not sappy or superficial) and they had to say, in a big way, Thank You Very Much.

That's when the second part of the study kicked in. Professor Toepfer's students were asked to assess their own mood and general satisfaction with life, right after each letter was written.

The results were remarkable. Every student reported increased levels of happiness after completing their assignment. Three-quarters of them volunteered that they would keep writing letters to people that mattered, even after the study was completed.

Professor Toepfer wasn't altogether surprised. "We're all walking around with an amazing resource: gratitude," he says. "It helps us express and enjoy, appreciate, be thankful and satisfied with a little effort. We all have it, and we need to use it to improve our quality of life."

Amen to that. I don't know about you, but I've got a Santa's sack worth of letters that are long overdue. To my parents, for starters (moved on, alas. No forwarding address). To a couple of old lovers, many old friends and more than a few enemies (as Bob Dylan wrote, "The cause was there before we came").

I owe at least a grateful postcard to that bouncer in the Yellowknife bar who let me know by the subtlest of eye contact and a certain squaring of his shoulders that it would be really wise of me to shut my yap, find my coat and make an early night of it. And of course I owe a letter to Mr. Nicholls.

My grade eleven English teacher. A large, sweet man who loved Shakespeare and tolerated, with pained grace, the unlettered barbarian hordes who slouched into his classroom. If I distinguished myself under Mr. Nicholls's tutelage, it was through wisecracks, spitballs, rude noises and crude snickers. I was, not to put too fine a point on it, a jerk. Mr. Nicholls ignored me. Then one day, he handed back an essay assignment. I can still see his note in the margin, written in spidery red ballpoint: "You certainly have a fine natural ability as a writer," it said.

News to me. I was the class screw-up. Useless at everything from geometry to gymnastics, from social studies to science. The caption under my photo in the school yearbook read: "Most Likely To Do Time."

But Mr. Nicholls's marginal comment was my tipping point. It tilted me toward a life of writing. Today, I can look back on twelve books, a career in radio, two television shows and thirty-plus years of writing newspaper columns and say, "It was all my English teacher's fault."

So Mr. Nicholls—whether you're still with us on earth or expounding on the looniness of Lear in some celestial lecture hall—a heartfelt Thank You.

And yes, I feel better already.